The Truth Behind The Mask

By

James Earl Smith

Acknowledgements

I truly acknowledge the gift of the Holy Spirit that has urged me for years to write this book. Putting it off till a later date, I can no longer do. As I notice the status of our deacons today, it hurts to see their limited amount of knowledge concerning the scriptures and the office in which they hold. Divisions flood the churches today and the deacons are unaware of how to solve the problems. In many cases, they're the ones who cause the problems and they're unaware of it. I hope that this book will be strength to them and guide them in the ways of truth. Deacons, it's time to listen to God's word. Open up your eyes and read for yourself and pray that God will open up your understandings. Listen to the words of King David, a man after God's own heart, who declares that the fear of the Lord is the beginning of wisdom (Psalm 111:10). The wisest man that ever lived went on to tell us wisdom is the principal thing; therefore get wisdom: and with all thy getting get understanding (Proverbs 4:7). In other words, they're telling us to get an understanding of what the responsibility of a deacon is and be sure you understand that you're not only making a commitment to the members of your church but you're also making a commitment to God. Be careful of the position you seek among God's people. Joshua points out that one cannot promise to serve the Lord, who is a holy and jealous God, while continuing in his/her sin nor return to his/her sinful ways and expect the Lord to overlook the transgressions nor sins one commits (Joshua 24).

The first thing every deacon should know is that the office in which he holds is a necessary, needful; inspired, and serious office. It is not one to be entered into blindly. It has its benefits; it has its downfalls. One should be aware of the responsibilities and expectations of the office before entering into it. The scriptures clearly list the qualifications a man should possess before even being considered for the office but few, if any, bothers to read them. Satan has deceived many people and leaders into believing that no man can be qualified according to God's written qualifications but if God inspired the apostle Paul to write them then there're men qualified to fit them. Does this mean that a man must be perfect? No, it only means that his life style must line up with biblical qualifications. Don't allow other people to force you into something you know you're not ready or qualified for. If you desire the office, start preparing yourself to fall in line with what God requires you to be in scripture.

Being ignorant is not an excuse. If one accepts the appointment, one accepts the responsibilities surrounding the office.

Before accepting the vow to serve as a deacon, or any other church leader, consider what Ecclesiastes 5:4-5 says about a vow. When thou vow a vow unto God, defer (**hesitate**) not to pay it; for *he hath* no pleasure in fools: pay that which thou hast vowed. Better *is it* that thou should not vow, than that thou should vow and not pay. It's simply tells us to perform the duties of the office we've willingly accepted before God and man. Whereas man may turn a deaf ear to your failure to be faithful, God will not.

Table of Contents

Part 1

The Truth from Behind the Mask

Introduction

The New Testament church was established on the day of Pentecost as the Holy Ghost filled the room where the apostles abode. It gave them the ability to speak in tongues that they had never spoken in before. The inhabitants of Jerusalem heard and saw what was going on and were truly amazed. Many had their opinions of what was happening but only Peter and the rest of the apostles new the truth of what was happening (Acts 2:14-33). They knew because they had been taught the scriptures by their Lord and Savior, Jesus Christ, before He ascended up into the heavens.

Today, it amazes me when I see so many men and women in the pulpit that have never been in a Sunday school class or have ever received any teaching or learning of scripture at all yet they stand in a position trying to tell others about a God that they themselves know nothing about. They remind me of Simon, the man who used sorcery to bewitch the people of Samaria into thinking he was a man of God. Simon used sorcery but the unlearned, unconverted, leaders today uses the things mama and grandma said and did and somehow, they manage to bewilder the people just as Simon did. So many people like knowledge concerning the word of God. Most, if not all, church goers have their diver and expensive bibles but few ever read or study them. Knowledge is available yet so many who pretend to be Christians will perish because they have rejected it (Hosea 4:6). They cannot discern between the gospel, which is the good news about Jesus Christ, and gossip, which is everything but the gospel.

Men and women accept positions in the church not knowing what the office means or calls for, the responsibility of the office, the qualification required for the office, or the expectations of God concerning the office. They think only of the title and benefits, never considering the devotion to the service or the penalty for failure to live up to the expectations of the office. My fellow deacons there's a penalty for our neglect of duty whether we know it or not. *(1 Cor. 5: 10)" For we must all appear before the judgment seat of Christ, that each one may receive the things done in the body, according to what he has done, whether good or bad."* We are urged to study the scriptures (2 Tim. 2:15). By studying the scriptures, we learn how to equip ourselves for the office we desire to fill. The scriptures are our guide to faithfulness. *2 Tim. 3: 16-17, " All scripture is given by inspiration of God, and is profitable for doctrine, for reproof, for correction, for instruction in righteousness, that the man of God may be complete, thoroughly equipped for every good work."*

All true believers are endowed with the Holy Spirit. God speaks to them and through them just as he said he would Heb.8:12.

 Some ministers think God only speaks through them but this is not true. God speaks to and through every believer that has the gift of the Holy Spirit dwelling in his/her heart. The scripture tells us that the spirit of God is alive; therefore it grows. It is not alive in the preacher and dead in the deacon or lay person. Notice what it did in Acts chapter 6 verses 7 and 8. After the seven received the laying on of hands, the word of God spread, and the number of the disciples multiplied greatly in Jerusalem. The spirit caused Stephen to do great wonders and signs. On the day of Pentecost, the spirit gave the apostles the ability to speak in languages different than their native language. At Cornelius house, when the spirit fell upon them great joy was seen. The Gentiles were given the gift of the Holy Spirit which increased their knowledge of the living God (Acts 10:44-45). Whenever the spirit enters a heart, it inspires movement. Whether it's in the preacher' heart or anyone else's, the spirit is alive. Jesus said it would be a teacher to us and a reminder of the things we've read, and been taught. He also said it would guide us in the ways of truth and would speak on behalf of the Father and Son (St. John chapters 14-16). Keep in mind also that Peter declares all believers to be of the royal priesthood.

I've more than once heard it said that Christ left the church in the hands of the seven Deacons. There is no truth to this statement anywhere in scripture.

Remember, we're told by scripture to prove all things and this is a statement that cannot be proven. The seven men found in Acts the 6th chapter through the 9th chapter were appointed to oversee the daily welfare needs of the widows in the congregation. However, they were in no way limited to that position. We should all strive to become greater servants in the Lord' service: five of the seven seemed to have been satisfied with just being over the daily provisions since nothing else is mentioned of them other than tradition. Stephen and Philip set their goals on becoming more. Stephen went on to become a preacher. Philip went on to preach, heal, do signs and wonders, baptized, and became a Missionary.

Even today, there are those deacons who are satisfied with just being able to carry on the devotion service of the church. Some seem to think that raising and counting the finance fulfills their service as a deacon. Others strive to become more; some set their goals on the teaching ministry, prison ministry, the outreach ministry, and some even goes on to be ministers of the gospel as Stephen and Philip did. Jesus said to his disciples," *the harvest truly is plenteous, but the laborers are few. Pray ye therefore the Lord of the harvest, that he will send forth laborers into the harvest."*(St. Mat. 9: 37-38) There's plenty of work to be done and the church needs all of us working together to get it done. It's not a one man' job; It's not a one group's job but a job for all the members working together as one for the edification of the body

Since this book's main aim is to strengthen the knowledge and understanding of the office of the deacon, defining what a deacon is should be the first step. A deacon is a servant as is all other members of the church including ministers and pastors; if the seven men in acts the 6th chapter were actually deacons, **(though in the book of Acts they're not called deacons)** then, the deacon's duty is clear. They were chosen to serve the widows, not the congregation, not the apostles or preachers. Tradition has taught us that in any and every established organization whether state, federal, religious, or other, problems and conflicts will arise from time to time. In fact, Jesus tells us in St. Luke 17:1a it is impossible but that offences will come. Wisdom, if sought and followed, will instruct us how to confront them. This is what the apostles did to restore unity back to the congregation. They moved with the guidance of the Holy Spirit, which Jesus, their Lord, had told them would guide them in all things (St. John 14:26).

The apostles were commissioned by the Holy Spirit to first address the multitude to offer a solution toward solving the up roar. They instructed the brethren to look among the multitude and find seven men of honest report full of wisdom and the Holy Ghost that they could appoint over the business. The apostles left the choosing of these men solely in the hand of the brethren **(the church)**. By the example set forth by the apostles from the beginning of the church, the apostles or preachers should have nothing to do with selecting or choosing men for the office of deaconship or stewardship. It is the responsibility of the church to choose and the responsibility of the pastors to ordain men to the office but only after they have made sure the men clearly understand the responsibilities, duties, and faithfulness require by the church and God regarding the office. These men selected in the book of Acts **(whether they were to be deacons or trustees)** were to be and were appointed as overseers, not helpers, of the administration. In other word, they were to be in complete charge of the administration. Their loyalty, faithfulness, and the gift of the Holy Spirit, seen within them, were the signs that showed their trustworthiness for the office. The apostles realized their hands were full with the responsibility they were chosen to fulfill. In the book of 1 Cor.12: 4-11 we read of the many spiritual gifts that God has placed in the church. *Now there are diversities of gifts,* *but the same Spirit. And there are differences of administrations but the same Lord. And there are diversities of operations, but it is the same God which worketh all in all. But the manifestation of the Spirit is given to every man to profit withal. For to one is given by the Spirit the word of wisdom; to another the word of knowledge by the same Spirit; to another faith by the same Spirit; to another the gifts of healing by the same Spirit; to another the working of miracles; to another prophecy; to another discerning of spirits; to another **divers** kinds of tongues; to another the interpretation of tongue: but all these work that one and the selfsame Spirit, dividing to every man severally as he will.* No one man or woman is the church. No one man or woman runs the church. No one man or woman has the gifts to fulfill all the necessary offices needed in the church. When every level of government in the church fulfills their function, all the members are sufficiently cared for but when one man or one group try to run the whole church all the members suffers.

In the world through much profit and gain, we can earn a big name. In the church through faithful service and devotion, we can earn a good name. In the world, a big name can make us rich and powerful but a good name in the service of the Lord can earn us peace of mind and eventually salvation. Which would you prefer a big name to gain you worldly fame or a good name that you, God, and others, will always cherish?

The Role of Leadership

The role of leadership is to lead by example not by words. In order to lead one needs the virtues of wisdom, understanding, and obedient. The gift of leadership derived from the ability to follow. One' obedient to follow will one day make him/her a wise leader. For how can one lead, except he/she be taught. King Solomon, the wisest man that ever lived, realized this after ascending the throne behind his father, David. He sought an answer from the source of all wisdom. In (1 King 3:6-9, 29) he asked wisdom for understanding to judge and lead God' people. In verse 29, God gave Solomon not only wisdom but exceedingly great understanding. The first thing one needs for Christian leadership is wisdom. Not worldly wisdom but spiritual wisdom which can only come from God. (James 1:5) *if any of you lacks wisdom, let him ask of God, who gives to all liberally and without reproach, and it will be given to him.* This is not a truth the apostle James is making to the world; he is speaking to God' people scattered abroad. *Psalms 111:10) the fear (reverence) of the Lord is the beginning of wisdom and a good understanding have all those who do his commandments.*

In Proverbs 9:10 Solomon repeats his father' words. *The fear of the Lord is the beginning of wisdom and the knowledge of the Holy One is (an) understanding:*

The key things that every leader need are wisdom, understanding, and obedient, guided by the Holy Spirit. The wisest man that ever lived was inspired by the Holy Spirit to leave these words on record as a guide to leadership in future generations. He tells us there's security in wisdom. Read Proverbs 4:5a, 7. *Get wisdom! Get (an) understanding!* In verse 7, he goes on to say, *wisdom is the principle thing: therefore get wisdom and in all thou getting get (an) understanding.* Understanding means knowing and putting things in their right relationship. The old folk would call it common sense. Wisdom is defined as knowledge guided by understanding.

How do we get wisdom? (John 8:31-32) *if you abide in my word, you are my disciples indeed (work) and you shall know the truth and the truth shall make you free.* (John 5:39) *Search the scriptures, for in them you think you have eternal life: and these are they which testify of me.* (2 Timothy 2:15) *Study to show thyself approved unto God, a workman that needs not to be ashamed, rightly dividing the word of truth*: these are just a few of the scriptures that point to the fact that one must study God' words in order to gain the wisdom of the truth leaders should be following after. Once we learn the truth for ourselves, we will no longer have to rely on what mama, big mama, the old warriors, or the preacher said. We'll know the truth for ourselves. There are many sayings the bible has been accused of saying that's not true. If leaders and other God fearing men and women would take the time to search the scriptures, they'd find whether they are qualified for the role of leadership. Every leader need to be taught prior to his/her office of appointment and continue being taught after accepting the role. Much of that teaching will come from the Lord through the teaching and guidance of the Holy Spirit but some will come from other individuals God has inspired to give you counsel. Jethro gave Moses counsel and by following it, it relieved pressure off of Moses and the people by co-sharing the work of leadership. (Exodus 18; 17-23) Aquila and Priscilla gave Apollos counsel and he became a more powerful speaker. (Acts 18:26-28) Rahab counseled the two spies and their lives were spared. (Joshua 2:12-24)

Now, let's go back to Psalms 111:10, and Proverbs 9:10. We get wisdom by getting knowledge of the Holy One through keeping his commandments. Before taking on a leadership role of any kind, a person should go through a period of been taught. The apostles were taught by Jesus. Paul was taught by Gamaliel Acts 22:3 and later by the disciples at Damascus acts 9:6-20. Timothy was taught by his mother, Eunice, and grandmother, Lois, in 2 Tim. 1:5. Timothy, Titus, Silas, and others also received teachings from the apostle Paul as indicated by the letters he wrote to the different churches he wrote too. Moses was taught by God on Mount Sinai and through the wilderness journey. Carefully read Exodus, Leviticus, Numbers, and Deuteronomy.

Although it is essential for leaders to receive knowledge before assuming leadership roles in the church, wisdom without the guidance of the Holy Spirit is fruitless. Paul' knowledge of Jewish law far surpassed that of many of his peers, but without the knowledge and guidance of the Holy Spirit, he became a destroyer of the churches of the Lord rather than a builder. After the encounter on the

Damascus road, and being baptized by Ananias, Paul received the Holy Spirit and his entire life style changed. *Moses was learned in all the wisdom of the Egyptians, and was mighty in words and in deeds.* (Acts 7:22) Moses sought to use his earthly wisdom and power to deliver his brethren but he made a mistake and had to flee for his life Acts7:24-29 but when he encountered the angel of the Lord in the burning bush and was commissioned by God to return to Egypt he went back with the knowledge of God and the guidance of the Holy Spirit, equipped to lead his brethren out of Egyptian bondage Exodus 3-12. The apostle received at least three years of instructions from Jesus and yet they did not understand his mission on earth. (Acts 1:6) After they received the gift of the Holy Spirit on the day of Pentecost, the Holy Spirit opened up their understanding. The Ethiopia eunuch was a man of great authority and one who read the scriptures but without the gift of the Holy Spirit, he was clueless to their meanings. (Acts 8:27-40) so you see, one may be in leadership, with or without the knowledge of the word, void of the Holy Spirit, his/her knowledge will still be fruitless.

Those in leadership should never become partakers of other men sins. (1 Tim. 5:22) *lay hands suddenly on no man, neither be partaker of other men's sins; keep thyself pure.* Partaker means to share in. So often leaders allow kinship, friendship, and courtship to cloud their judgment in decision making: When a leader supports or turns a deaf ear to wrong doing in the church because he don't want to offend a friend, relative, or partner, he becomes a partaker of that person' sin. Leadership has a responsibility to discipline all wrong doings. (2 Tim. 4:1-2) *I charge thee therefore before God, and the Lord Jesus Christ, who shall judge the quick and the dead at his appearing and his kingdom; preach the word; be instant in season, out of season; reprove, rebuke, exhort with all long-suffering and doctrine.* Leaders must learn how to rebuke and reprove a person' evil nature but love the person. You cannot do this by allowing a person to remain in a position when you know the person' life is not in order for leadership. How can a God fearing leader justify himself by placing a gay person, adulterer, bigamist, fornicator, or other evil doer, in a position in the church? (Gal. 5:19-22) God does not commission the unsaved to teach the unsaved how to be saved. (Mat. 15:14a) *If the blind lead the blind, both shall fall into the ditch*. As leaders, avoid getting entangled with the opposite sex, proverbs 6:32. *Whoever commits adultery with a woman lacks understanding: he who does so destroys his own soul.* Getting into relationships with women, or men if the leader is female, will eventually come to the light and the confident people have in you will be scattered, if not destroyed, and the formal confident will never be retained. Supporting things like money, sex, friendship, and kinship in ways that are evil can gain you and the one you're supporting a space in hell. At some point, every leader should be able to say like Paul (1 Cor.11:1) *"Be ye followers of me even as I also am of Christ. (1 Tim. 4:12) Let no man despise your youth, but be an example to the believers in words, in conduct, in love, in spirit, in faith, in purity, till I come give attention to reading, to exhortation, to doctrine.* Leaders should lead by examples as Jesus did in St. John 13:12-15.

Let's compare what Solomon needed to what the leaders under Moses needed to what the seven men of Acts 6 needed. Solomon asked for understanding and was given understanding and great wisdom because of his obedient. The leadership under Moses was to be (Exodus 18:21) able men, (men who had proven themselves) such as fear God (men of wisdom) remember (prov.9:10) the fear of the Lord is the beginning of wisdom. Men of truth, hating covetousness (trustworthy men) in Acts 6, the apostles called for men of honest report, (men who have proven themselves) full of the Holy Ghost and wisdom (men of wisdom guided by the Holy Spirit) in 1Tim 3:8-13 the deacon is to be one of good report (not a drunker, not greedy for money, a man that takes care of and rules his family well by being an example to them in all things. Not double-tongued (He must be trustworthy, his words must be dependable) holding the mystery of the faith in a good conscience (filled with the Holy Spirit). When we examine these four areas of leadership, we see much the same requirements for leadership. (1) Honesty (2) wisdom and understanding (3) knowledge of the Holy One (or Holy Spirit)

One of the greatest dangers in the church today is mechanical instruments. Worldly toys, that the world has convinced us is a necessity of life, Things like cell phones, tablets, Ipads, and the likes. There's nothing wrong with the usage of these things in their proper place but the church is not the proper place. Why? They provide an environment of misconception. While some are following the minister in his text, others are on the internet, or texting their friend, watching a movie, playing games, or etc. Nobody is the wiser of what's going on. If everyone was using their bibles, there'd be no misconception of what people were reading or viewing.

Another thing I've noticed is the rise in scriptural translations; there're many available today. In every congregation, there're diver people using diver translations when it should be encouraged that everyone used the same translation. Paul outlines the order of worship in (1 Cor. 14:26). *How is it then, brethren? When ye come together, every one of you hath a psalm, hath a doctrine, hath a tongue, hath a revelation, hath an interpretation. Let all things be done unto edifying.* He encourages everyone in the same congregation to use the same doctrine. (The same scriptural translation)

The Truth as Written

For decades, ministers and pastors have kept deacons in the dark concerning what the bible says about the office of the deacon. When training deacons, they refer them to deacon' books, written, explained, and outlined, mainly by ministers, which keeps the deacon in the dark concerning his position and function in the church. Keeping the deacon in the dark concerning his role in the church robs him of the true work he is called to perform. Since he is a co-worker in the support of the gospel, his work is essential.

First, let's see what the bible says compared to what the preachers say. Turn your bible to acts 6th chapter and begin reading with the first verse. It tells you that when the church grew in number problems began to rise among some of the believers (disciples). This problem extended from those in charge of making sure the widows were cared for on an equal basis. The people who were over this administration were not faithful in their duties. It seems they, apparently Jewish overseers, were only concerned about making sure the widows of their nationality were taken care of and had no true feeling concerning the Grecians converts. If you take note, you'll see that this was the first interruption of the new established church but so serious it divided the church and stopped its growth. *Acts.4:32 (all that believed were of one heart.)* This first sin or division that arose within the church resulted when those in charge showed "respect of person" between the Grecian and Hebrew widows. This sin of respect of person is one that continues to pledge our churches today. Although we hear it mentioned often, we fail to practice what we preach. James 2:1 tells us not to have the faith of our Lord Jesus Christ, **the** Lord of glory, with respect of person. Yet, when it's shown in the church today, we witness the same effect on the congregation as it had on the early church. If we find ourselves performing this act, we should immediately refrain from it before it causes divisions among the congregation. When problems arise in the church, the sooner we confront them, the less harm they're allowed to do. When the problem arose in the early church, the apostles immediately called the multitude of the disciples together and offered a solution to solving the problem (sin). Please note; the apostles (preachers) did not get involved with the problem. They met with the multitude of the disciples and told the brethren to choose seven men full of wisdom, the Holy Ghost, and of honest report and they, the apostles, would appoint them over the administration to deal with the problem. Here the apostles, guided by the Holy Spirit, realized that the ministers of God should never get involved with certain issues in the church but leave them to lesser appointees in the church. (1 Cor.6:4) *If ye then have judgments of things pertaining to this life, set (place) them to judge (to deal with the problem) who are least esteemed in the church* (not outside the church as some translations interpret this verse). Why did this problem need to be dealt with? Let's go to James 2:1 *(My brethren, have not the faith of our Lord Jesus Christ, the Lord of glory, with respect of persons.)* the following verses go on to tell us how showing difference between the members of the church is a sin. This sin is one of the most widely spread sin in the church today. It stunts the growth of the church today just like it did in the days of the apostles. If a problem is noticed and dealt with when it first begins, it'll cause little to no hurt to the body.

How often does leadership find or place people in their church congregation over the wrong auxiliary? Being nice does not qualify a person for a role of leadership in the church. Leadership roles have no power over making people faithful. How often do leadership allow good people, although faithful and devoted to the service they perform, to cause division among the auxiliary on which they serve, by doing things out of order? How do they rightfully distinguish between love and mercy? Is it Love when we leave a person in a position in which he/she cannot perform and allow his/her tenure to continue causing ill feelings among the congregation? Efforts to show what some call love and mercy often ends up being sin. Just because a person has the desire to do a good deed does not make it right especially if it's done in a manner that offends others. Selfishness (**having our own way no matter who it offends**) is not the way of a child of God. 1 Cor.8:9 and verses 12-13 says but take heed lest by any means this liberty (**freedom to act without being rebuked**) of yours become a stumbling block to them that are weak...when ye sin so against the brethren, and wound their weak conscience, ye sin against Christ. Paul says in verse thirteen wherefore, if meat (**his reference here not**

31

only refers to meats but any and all things that a Christian does or thinks of doing that offends or causes others to stumble.) makes my brother to offend, I will eat no flesh while the world stands, lest I make my brother to offend.

The sixth Chapter of Acts outlines the basic qualifications that all that desire to be or is appointed to be in leadership should possess (whether the desire is to be Pastor, minister, deacon, teacher, usher, or etc.). Let's go back to the book of Acts. Remember in the first chapters of the book of Acts, the members of the church were as one they had all things in common but the neglect of the widows caused a murmuring among the church and it had to be dealt with before the church could become again as one and continue to grow. Be sure you also read chapter 5, it tells you how togetherness promotes growth. The apostles saw that their plates were full with the teaching, and preaching of the word. They did not have time to watch over or get involved with the administration of serving food. So they were inspired by the Holy Spirit to call the multitude of disciples together, whereas they explained their position and place in the church, so they instructed the brethren to choose seven men from among the congregation that possessed qualities beneficial equally to the widows, the church and God. Someone they, **the apostles who were led by the Holy Spirit,** could appoint **over** the business. Not necessarily to do the actual serving but to make sure those who did would treat Jewish and Grecians widows as one. Why did the apostles want the brethren of the church to select them? Because they dwelt with them on a daily basic they knew who was faithful and who was not. They knew the life style of the men. The apostle did not. Notice they asked them to choose men they knew were of honest report, full of the Holy Ghost and wisdom. Seven men were to be chosen, not as a limitation to the number of men that can be chosen for office, but because seven were sufficient to handle this particular job. These men only needed three things to qualify them for this appointment. They had to be of honest report, full of the Holy Ghost and wisdom. These are the main virtues every church officer should possess before they are even considered for a leadership role in the church. These men were never called deacons nor is there any indication that they were deacons. In fact, if you look at the qualification of the deacon and the qualifications of these men you'll see that the deacon is held to a much higher standard than these men. However, pastors like to refer to them as being deacons to hold them to the position of table servers.

Open up your eyes and minds that you can see, read, and hear the truth about this matter. These men were place over the welfare administration of the widows in the church which was a common practice of the church to take care of those who had given their lives serving the church and its members. *(1 Tim: 5:9-10) Let not a widow be taken into the number under threescore years old, having been the wife of one man, well reported of for their good works; if she have brought up children, if she have lodged strangers, if she have washed the saints' feet, if she have relieved the afflicted, if she have diligently followed every good work.* These were widows (only women qualified) who had no husbands, children or grandchildren to care for them. This practice of feeding widows in the church became obsolete many decades ago. If these men were deacons and the deacon' duty is solely to wait on tables serving the hungry, then the deacon' duty became obsolete, when the church ceased from this practice.

These men were never labeled as deacons. Go back to Acts the sixth chapter first verse and you'll see that the people in charge were not trustworthy. That's why the problem arose. That's also why the apostles asked for faithful men full of the Holy Ghost and wisdom, trustworthy men (trustees) who would see to it that everyone was treated equally in the daily administration. The apostles asked for trustworthy men not deacons. The bible never called them deacons. Only pastors, preachers, and deacons who refuse to read for themselves called or calls them deacons. Even if they were the fore runners of the deaconship, they were not chosen just to serve the needs of the widows but the Holy Spirit went on to enlist their services as co-workers in the ministry. The scripture clearly states that Stephen strait way preached the word showing signs and wonders among the people and became the first Christian' martyr. Philip went on to be a missionary; he preached the word and established the church in Samaria showing signs and wonders, and went on to baptize the Ethiopian Eunuch that is credited by some for the gospel being carried to Ethiopia. If we are to call these men deacons, then, by following what the scripture says, the deacon' duties are not limited. According to the gift given to the seven by the

Holy Spirit, some taught and preached, as Stephen and Philip did. Consider now what the scripture said of Stephen, strait way, he was empowered by the Holy Spirit to do these things. No leader can represent or serve God's people without the gift and guidance of the Holy Spirit. Philip on the other hand went down to Samaria; he preached, healed, baptized, did miracles, and became a missionary. These men did not serve or perform at the discretion of the Apostles. They were directed by the holy Spirit Acts. 6:8, 7:55, 8:5-7, 8:26, 8:39.

If these were deacons, at some point in life, we need to choose who we're going to believe. Some preachers say deacons were chosen to wait on tables only, but the scriptures do not state that these were deacons. Some of the old warriors and deacons say the number of deacons chosen should not exceed seven. Neither of these statements is supported by scripture. Prayerfully read Acts chapters 6 and 7. These seven were not only chosen to care for the needs of the aged church widows they were also chosen by the Holy Spirit to be co- workers in the gospel. Not only were they to oversee the care of those who were not able to care for themselves. The spirit added to that ministry by leading them (strait way) to take part in the ministry of healing, teaching, preaching, baptizing, counseling, (as Philip did unto the Eunuch), and supporting the Out Reach ministry to aid the needy whatever their needs may be. One of the basic jobs of the deacon today, as it has been for many generations, is to look out for the needs of the congregation. Whatever and whenever those needs come up, the deacons have always been available to handle them. This leaves the pastor free to consecrate solely on the spreading of the word and prayer as the apostles mentioned in Acts the sixth chapter. Preaching the gospel, prayer, and meditation, requires much study and time. Many things pastors must have the wisdom to understand that they should never get involved in. By considering and following the example of the first church leaders, (the apostles), much stress and ill feelings will be avoided. Notice the things the apostles said they would give themselves continually (**always)** to.

Again if the men of Acts the sixth chapter were deacons, then the deacon has many functions in the church. For sure, in this chapter the apostles point out their' (**the preacher's)** position in the church. Notice Acts

6:2b; *it is not reason that we should leave the word of God, and serve tables.* Verse four goes on to state *but we (***the apostles***) will give ourselves continually* **(without cessation or intermission; unceasingly)** *to prayer, and to the ministry of the word.* The deacon's duty may not be clearly defined in scripture but the apostles clearly outlined the duty of the pastors and ministers concerning their responsibility in the church. In a world where sin continues to rise, ministers for sure need to continue in prayer and the study of the word. As the atheistic continue to outlaw God's word and statures, ministers must stand firm in the knowledge of the word to feed their flock that they not stray from the right path.

A Vivid Look at the Bishop's Qualifications

Now let's go to 1st Timothy the third chapter and begin at the first verse. It gives you the qualification of the bishop as being one of being blameless, (**not a perfect man but one without false in the following qualifications**) the husband of one wife (**the members of the church, though many members, represent one body united under one head which is Christ. Marriage is symbolic of the church and the leader thereof must represent the oneness of the flesh as well as the oneness of the faith. The scripture says therefore shall a man leave his father and mother, and shall cleave unto his wife, not wives, and they shall be one flesh Genesis 2:24. A man and his wife can become as one but a man and his wives can never agree or be as one. Notice the conflict between Sarah and Hagar, Abraham' wives, the conflict between Rachel and Leah, Jacob' wives, the many wives of King Solomon, which eventually caused him to build idol temples which placed a strange on his people to build and support. Multiple wives can cause a strange on any marriage. Therefore, they can never be nor ever be represented as one flesh. In Malachi 3:6a, God says "For I** am the Lord, I change not." Hebrews 13:8 declares Jesus Christ the same yesterday, and today, and forever. We've come to believe that God and Christ never change but we fail to realize that Satan is also an unchanging evil being. The same method of deception he used on Eve he continues to use on mankind today. Roman 3:23 has become a crutch that Satan has inspired us to use when we want to justify our sins of omission and commission. Wrong is wrong no matter who does it and leaders have a charge to say so even if they themselves have committed it 2 Tim. 4:1-5. Romans 3:23 does not justify men sins but Roman 6:23 does declare their ending.) The bishop must be vigilant. (He must always be awake and alert, and keenly watchful to ward off danger or trouble from his flock. His concern for his flock must be seen through his love and devotion to them.)He must be sober. (He must be one who is quiet in demeanor not playful but one that possess a quality of seriousness. If he is to stand and represent the true and living God, his character must be the picture of authority.) A bishop must be of good behavior. (The scripture says that the servant of God must not strive; but be gentle to all men 2 Tim. 2:24. His conduct must always be orderly. In word, in conversation, in charity, in spirit, in faith and in purity, his behavior must be exemplary 1 Tim. 4:12.) Never should he disgrace himself in an argumentative or childish manner. The bishop must be one given to hospitality. (His reception and entertainment of strangers must always be friendly. His warm and gentle nature should light up his character.) The bishop must be apt to teach. Not only should the bishop have a desire to teach he must also be fit and capable of teaching. He too must be teachable. The man who is not teachable has a closed mind to wisdom. When this happens, he has to rely on pride and ego. These are arrogances that can cause him and his followers to suffer.) The bishop must be one not given to wine. The bishop must not be a heavy drinker in fact it would be better if leaders did not drink at all. Proverbs 20:1 says wine *is* a mocker, strong drink *is* raging: and whosoever is deceived thereby is not wise. The first known drunker was Noah. Heavy drinking uncovered a part of him that was not decent. It has been proven that heavy drinking causes a person to say and do things that can be devastating to his character. A bishop must be careful not to allow his desire for things like wine to place him in the snare of the devil. A bishop must not be a striker. **The bishop must not be a striker or contentious man. He must avoid being in quarrelsome controversies. Being a leader, he must avoid getting into arguments. It only takes one misguided confrontation to smear his good name and cause slander to his profession. 2 Tim. 2:24 Points out that the servant of the Lord must not strive; but be gentle unto all men.** The bishop must not be greedy of filthy lucre. **If money is his goal, spiritually, his congregation will suffer. A bishop' main aims should be to preach the gospel of Jesus Christ, warn sinners of their sin and draw them to the one that has the power to save their soul (Jesus Christ).** Paul tells young Timothy to *flee from those who are greedy and want to become wealthy from the ministry. 1 Tim: 6: 5-11* (New King James Bible) instead of being covetous for worldly gain, he should be a patient man. **One who patiently waits on his reward knowing his God will supply his every need. He should be a man who serves without complaint or anger. He should be one, like the apostles, who dedicates himself to prayer and the spreading of the word.** A bishop of the Lord cannot be a brawler. **It is unseemly to see a bishop bickering and arguing like the unsaved sinner. His appearance and character should** always be exemplary. Even when confronting the ungodly, the sword of the spirit must be used in love. The man that represents the Lord must not be covetous. **The bishop must not allow Satan to beguile him as he did Eve. He must not be covetous of money, women, pride, or any other ungodly desires.** He has to be one that rules **(manages)** well his own house, having his children in subjection **(under godly control)** with all gravity **(dignity and respect).** For if a man know not how to rule his own house, how shall he take care of the church of God? **A bishop must have the ability to rule his own children. This will have a bearing on his ability to rule the church of God. If those you feed and cloths within your own household have no respect or honor for you, how can you expect others to do so?** A novice **(one who is a beginner in the ministry should never be chosen as a bishop (leader) of a church.** promoting a person to leadership too soon can easily lift one up with pride. Proverbs 16:18 says pride *goes* before destruction, and a haughty spirit before a fall. Placing a beginner at the head of a church congregation is sure to cause the beginner to grow in arrogance and the congregation to suffer. A bishop must be an example to the flock he watches over.

He must also have a good report of them which are in the world to avoid heresies from being spread that could cause slander to his tenure.

The Scriptural Qualifications of the Deacon

Before we view the qualifications of the deacons, let's get one thing clear in our mind. The bible does not outline the duties of the deacon; it only outlines the spiritual qualifications. Compare Acts the sixth chapter with first Timothy three. The men in Acts were not subject to trial before appointment; they were appointed solely on the recommendation of the brethren. The men in first Timothy three were to be subject to approval before they could be allowed to use the office. Acts the sixth chapter called for honest men full of the Holy Ghost and wisdom. Honest men were needed because it had been proven that the men who were previously in charge were unfaithful in their duty. In fact, it was their unfaithfulness that caused the uproar. The men needed the Holy Ghost and wisdom to keep them humble and obedient leading them to fear God and serve their fellow man with grace and truth without showing respect of person. Their main duty was plain; it was to make sure all the widows of the church receive their daily welfare needs. Their duty had nothing to do with the needs of the congregation only the widows. However, if there's division among one section of the church, grievance is felt by the whole congregation. First Corinthians twelve twenty-six says *and whether one member suffers, all the members suffer with it; or one member be honored, all the members rejoice with it.* If the seven were chosen to look after the welfare of the widows and the preachers (apostles) were solely giving themselves to prayer and the ministry of the word, who was left to care for the other needs of the church? No minister or deacon has stopped to consider this question. Who was taking care of the finance? Who was taking care of the sick and poor of the congregation that were not widows? Who was taking care of the devotion and other service needs of the church? The answer can only be the same group the apostles told to choose the seven, the brethren and elders. Remember, when the murmuring got started, the apostles called the multitude (all the disciples, women and men) together but they then asked the brethren of the congregation to choose the seven. Choose them that they, the apostles, could appoint them over the care of the aged widows. I also ask you to notice that it was not the widows that started the murmuring but others in the congregation that was concerned about their well beings.

Let's look at another point in question. When the apostles told the brethren to choose men from among themselves to be appointed over the welfare needs of the widows and that they, the apostles, had no reason to intermeddle in that administration of the church, the saying pleased the whole multitude Acts :2-5. Even today, most church people prefer that pastors stay clear of the business issues in the church and place more interest in things like prayer, Sunday school, visitation, counseling, baptizing, and preaching the true gospel that convicts the sin in the life of the believer and sinner man as well.

The scripture declares that God has set some in the church. Notice it says God not man. First apostles, secondarily prophets, **(preachers)** thirdly teachers, after that miracles, then gifts of healings, helps, governments, **(groups to manage various areas of the church, the deacon board serves today as it has for hundreds of years as a presiding governing body),** and diversities of tongues (1 Cor.12:28): 1Cor. 12:5-6 Points out that there are differences of administrations, but the same Lord; and there are diversities **(many)** of operations, but it is the same God which works all in all. When will we ever learn to consult what God says and get away from what man says. If we accept what God says, we will never go wrong. At some point, Christian must learn to stand firm on God's word, like Peter and John did before the Jerusalem counsel. "Whether it is right in the sight of God to hearken unto you **(men)** more than unto God, judge ye. For we cannot but speak the things which we have seen and heard Acts 4:19b-20. Every level of government in the church has a function and purpose. In Acts 6:4, the apostles pointed out that their responsibility was to continue focusing their time on prayer and the ministry of the word. In Acts 6:1-3, we see where the seven were given the responsibility of watching over the daily administration of the aged widows. In Acts 6:2-5, we see it is the entire congregation responsibility to either agree or disagree on recommendations brought before them. We see in Acts 6:3, it is the Brethren responsibility to choose people with the right qualification and ability to fill the office they're being considered for. It was the Widows responsibility to set an example for the younger women in the way to bring up children, in the lodging of strangers, the washing of the saints' feet, and in relieving the afflicted 1 Tim.5:10.

In our churches today, we have deacon boards, usher boards, trustee boards, diver auxiliaries, committees in charge of various activities, today' church is ran by diver administrations. Each has its function. Each has its responsibility. All of the administrations should works toward the same common goal. That goal is to work in harmony and unity to bring sinners to the Lord. When the church chose men and women according to scripture qualification, the church will grow spiritually. When the church choses to disregard scriptural qualifications, it stunt its ability to grow and floods its self with divisions.

Now let's look at the qualification of the deacon according to the bible not according to leaders who seem to only want men who fall in line with their agenda. Verse 8 likewise (in similarity to the qualification of the bishop, in the same manner as the bishop) likewise must the deacon be:

1. He must be grave, (dignified and respectful). He should be one that respects the church and the

Lord in all that he says or does. He should be serious about the office he holds and the service of the office that has been entrusted unto him by God and the church. He will not be a perfect man but he must equip his life style to fit scriptural qualifications. After accepting the office of deaconship, one should realize that his life style will be constantly viewed and talked about. The deacon should do all within his powers to promote the growth of the church and avoid being an offender.

2. He must not be double-tongued (two-faced, or hypocritical) he must be a man who is trustworthy not a man who says one thing to one person and another to someone else. What he agrees to behind closed doors he should be man enough to face up to when standing before the congregation.

3. He must not be given too much wine. (Addicted to wine) Prov.20:1 says *"wine is a mocker, strong drink is a brawler, and whosoever is led astray by it is not wise."* One who holds the office of a deacon should be sober in all his ways.

4. He must not be greedy of filthy lucre (a lover of money) a deacon cannot be a man whose love for money causes him to stoop to ungodly means to acquire it. He must also understand that the church is not a business nor can it be run like a business. A business goal is the gain and profit of money or material assets using whatever means necessary. The church's goal is to equip souls for eternal life through spiritual virtues. The church is a living organism that needs love, faith, prayer, truth, and like virtues to grow. Though, there're many, many, Christian churches on earth, all fall under the head of Jesus Christ. In order to properly fulfill its goal, those who hold office in the local churches must be trustworthy and guided by the Holy Ghost and wisdom.

5. He must be a man who holds the mystery of the faith in a pure conscience. (His life style should justify his profession of Christianity. 1Tim: 4: 12 points out that leaders should be an example to the believers in words, conduct, love, spirit, faith, and in purity.

Only church leaders who are worthy of the office should be chosen. (1 Tim: 1-15) many who holds the office of deacons at their church have never even read the scriptures concerning the deacon' qualification or life style. They fail to realize the danger of accepting positions in which they're not qualified according to God' standards, those who accept positions they know nothing about or intends to live up too, lie to the people of their congregation and to God not realizing the final penalty. (Acts 5: 3-7)

If you'd notice, each virtue says, he must; not he should be, but must be, equipped with all of these virtues before he is allowed to use the office of the deacon. 1 Tim. 3:10 says let these (virtues) also first be proved then let them use the office of the deacon being found blameless (their character should be without accusation). The deacons are to be evaluated, observed, and approved before being appointed to office. Some leaders will tell you no men exist with these qualities today. I've learned that people usually judge others faithfulness by their own. Choosing proper men for the deacon ship depends on the members faithfulness to God words, the Word has declared what to look for in a man. The men who hold this office must be respectable at home, work, church, and elsewhere who always carry themselves in an up standing and dignified manner. Being a man in gender does not qualify one to be a deacon. So many churches and some pastors elect men thinking placing them in positions will make them become the men God want them to be. They ignore the fact that God words says they must be qualified before placing them in office. It is hypocritical to place people in office when you know they're not qualified to be there but people will place them there then criticize them for not performing the duties required concerning the office in which they've been placed in. The deacon of first Timothy three' worthiness is to be proven before being allowed to serve. If the church follow God's word in their selection, both the deacon and church will be blessed by his tenure. If it follows man's opinions or desires, as so many do today, the church will suffer as a result of its own mistake. In order for the church to grow, those in charge must be filled with the Holy Spirit. When we choose men according to God's word, God will crown them with the gift of the Holy Spirit. When we reject God's word, God rejects us. Scripture teaches us that qualification must be considered and observed before placing a person in office. Satan has deceived many church goers to believe that you can place a person in office and the office will make a person what he/she is not. Churches reject God's choice of people but pray to God to accept their choices. The seed we place in office, if it's according to God's word, will prosper. If it's not according to God's word, evil will catch root and spread.

The Deacon and his Wife

Now let's take a further step into the life of the men chosen for the deaconship. Not only are the men for the deaconship required to be faithful, their wives are also expected to be of Christian standards. Verse 11: *Even so must their wives be grave, not slanderers, sober, faithful in all things.* This verse deserves careful consideration because it states that the virtues of the wives must also be respectable for the man to be fit for the deaconship. Let's consider those virtues one by one.

1. Like their husbands, they must be grave. They must be dignified, serious, respectable, and honest in all things. *Eph. 5: 22, 24: wives submit yourselves unto your own husband as unto the Lords. Therefore as the church is subject unto Christ, let the wives be to their own husbands in everything. Col: 3:18 Says, "Wives, submit yourselves unto your own husbands, as it is fit in the Lord".*

2. They cannot be slanderers. They must not be guilty or have a reputation of being a hell raiser or one who spreads malicious gossip motivated by vicious

or mischievous purposes. *Eph:4: 31 "let all bitterness, and wrath, and anger, and clamor, and evil speaking, be put away from you, with all malice:"*

3. They are to be sober. They are to be understanding, discreet, temperate, and of a sound mind.

4. Faithful in all things: in dress *(1 Tim: 2: 9-12) in like manner also, that women adorn themselves in modest apparel, with shamefacedness and sobriety; not with braided hair, or gold, or pearls, or costly array.* The deacons and bishops wives should always be properly dressed. Their dresses should never be half way up their thighs nor should they wear low cut blouses, exposing too much of their bodies. They should also limit the amount of jewelry and make-up they wear. *Verse 10 and 11 but (which become women professing godliness) with good works. Let the woman learn in silence with all subjection* (the state of being under another's control). Be under obedience, *(1 Cor.14:34 but let your women keep silence in the churches: for it is not permitted unto them to*

speak; but they are commanded to be under obedience, as also said the law. The dress, the altitude, the respect, the honor, and obedient of a leader' wife can either uplift or degrade her husband' position. She must show her reverence of him in all things.

Let the deacon be the husband of one wife. Marriage is symbolic of the church and those that are in leadership must represent the oneness of the flesh and faith. *(Gen: 2:24) Therefore shall a man leave his father and his mother, and shall cleave unto his wife: and they shall be one flesh. (Mat: 19: 6) wherefore, they are no more twain, but one flesh. What therefore god hath joined together, let not man put asunder. (Rom: 7 : 2) for the woman that hath a husband is bound by the law to her husband so long as he live; but if the husband be dead, she is loosed from the law of her husband.* If a man has more than one living wife he cannot represent the oneness of the faith. The scriptures clearly state that a man shall leave his father and mother, and shall cleave unto his wife, not wives, and they shall be one flesh.

Ruling their children and their houses well, the household of the deacon must be orderly. Their children must be discipline and respectable their wives must be honorable and the deacons life styles must not be painted with such things as the writing of bad checks, extortion, fornication, poor business dealings, or the inability to make rational decisions toward the family' well beings. The last thing we see here concerning the deacon is his reward for serving well. He will obtain good standing and great boldness in the faith. The congregation will admonish and praise men who serve well as deacons. Doing well will gain them confident when they stand before the judgment seat of Christ. *(2 Cor. 10) for we must all appear before the judgment seat of Christ, that each one may receive the things done in the body, according to what he has done, whether good or bad. (New Kings James version)* They will also obtain great boldness in the faith which will gain them assurance in their Christian walk. The deacon must always be careful how he relates to the members of the congregation. He holds a position of honor therefore he must carry himself always in a Christian manner that is fitting for the office. Although there're no duties outlined in scriptures for the deacon, his qualifications speak to the fact that the office is one held in great regards. The office of the deacon has survived for hundreds of years and has been an important entity to the growth of the church.

Up and until a few decades ago it was the deacons who held the church together and kept it on the right track. They led the church in song, prayer, and the various teaching ministries. Pastors only visited the local country churches once a month but the deacons were there each time the doors opened. The church, mainly under the stewardship of the deacons, would not have survived without the leadership of the deacons. Keep in mind that the deacons would not have been able to carry on the work of the ministry without the approval, guidance, support and spirit of the Lord. In the book of Acts when the counsel of the Pharisees wanted to over throw the ministry of the apostles, wisdom directed Gamaliel to stand up and speak. *Then stood there up one in the council, a Pharisee, named Gamaliel, a doctor of the law, had in reputation among all the people, and commanded to put the apostles forth a little space; and said unto them, ye men of Israel, take heed to yourselves what ye intend to* *do as touching these men. For before these days rose up Theudas, boasting himself to be somebody; to whom a number of men, about four hundred, joined themselves; who was slain; and all , as many as obeyed him, were scattered, and brought to nought. After this man rose up Judas of galilee, in the days of the taxing, and drew away much people after him: he also perished; and all, **even** as many as obeyed him, were dispersed. And now I say unto you, refrain from these men, and let them alone: for if this council or this work be of men, it will come to nought: but if it be of God, ye cannot overthrow it; lest haply ye be found even to fight against God.* If the deacon ministry was and is of God, it shall continue to stand and function the way God intended for it to function. Like the Jerusalem counsel, many pastors and deacon boards struggle with contention today unable to find common ground between them to work as co-workers for the furtherance of the gospel. Instead, each struggles for dominant control over God's people.

The deacon, as is the pastor, is a servant. Who they serve will determine their latter end. If Satan can keep God's people fighting among themselves, his efforts to gain followers will be successful. I praise those pastors and deacon boards that are able to work together in harmony. The apostles and the brethren in the Jerusalem church were able to work together and because of it many disciples were added to the church by the Lord daily (Acts 6:7).

Summary

How long will you continue to follow the popular opinion and deny God' words. Open up your eyes, look, read, and see what the word says. Compare it to what man says. When Paul went to Berea to preach to the people of Berea, they received his words with all readiness of mind but they searched the scriptures daily, to see if the things Paul preached was true.(Acts. 17: 10-11) Paul had no problems with them confirming his words to be true; in fact, he welcomed it. But people today are too unconcerned and lazy to read for themselves. *(Hosea 4:6) my people are destroyed for lack of knowledge: because thou hast rejected knowledge, I will also reject thee, that thou shalt be no priest to me: seeing thou hast forgotten the law of thou God, I will also forget thy children.* Notice *(1 Peter 2:9) "But ye are a chosen generation (the church) a royal priesthood, a holy nation, a peculiar people;"* if we belongs to Jesus Christ there should be something peculiar about our character, the way we walk, the way we talk, and how we get alone with others.

The first thing many church leaders and members encourage deacons to do is purchase and read a deacon's book. Have you ever noticed that most all deacon books are written by ministers and they all have conflicting opinions? Some ministers, not all, outline the deacon duty to fit their personal agenda. They base their opinions and desires upon dictatorship authority rather than the mutual unity of sharing the responsibility of church government as the apostles did in Acts 6. The Holy Spirit led them to realize that the leadership role of the church was too vast for one group of persons to handle. The Holy Spirit directed them to ask the brethren of the church to select faithful men from among the congregation that could manage the needs of the aged widows. They (the apostles) saw no reason to get involved with the administration but felt it more important to give all of their attention to prayer, and the ministry of the word. Notice how this suggestion of the Holy Spirit caused great joy among the people. It took the stress off the apostles, allowed others to share in the ministry, gave the people the opportunity to choose the government they wanted to govern the affairs from among their own group, and it left the apostles free to serve in the capacity they were chosen for.

In the book of Exodus, The Holy Spirit directed Jethro, Moses father-in-law, to suggest a similar plan to Moses to relieve the stress off of Moses and the people he led. *(Exodus 18: 13- 26) And so it was, on the next day, that Moses sat to judge the people; and the people stood before Moses from morning until evening. So when Moses' father-in-law saw all that he did for the people, he said, "What is this thing that you are doing for the people? Why do you alone sit, and all the people stand before you from morning until evening?" And Moses said to his father-in-law, "Because the people come to me to enquire of God. When they have a difficulty, they come to me, and I judge between one and another; and I make known the statutes of God and His laws." So Moses father-in-law said to him, "The thing that you do is not good. Both you and these people who are with you will surely wear yourselves out. For this thing is too much for you; you are not able to perform it by yourself. Listen now to my voice; I will give you counsel and God will be with you: stand before God for the people, so that you may bring the difficulties to God. And you shall teach them the statutes and the laws, and show them the way in which they must walk and the work they must do. Moreover you shall select from all the people able men, such as fear God, men of truth, hating covetousness*; and place *such over them to be rulers of thousands, rulers of hundreds, rulers of fifties, and rulers of tens. And let them judge the people **at all times**. Then it will be that every great matter they shall bring to you, but every small matter they themselves shall judge. So it will be easier for you, for they will bear the burden with you. If you do this thing, **and God so commands you**, then you will be able to endure, and all the people will also go to their place in peace."* So Moses heeded the voice of his *father-in-law, and did all that he said. And Moses chose able men of all Israel, and made them heads over the people: rulers of thousands, rulers of hundreds, rulers of fifties, and rulers of tens. So they judged the people **at all times**; the hard cases they brought to Moses, but they judged every small case themselves.* We see it lightened the load of Moses giving him more time to meditate and consecrate on God and his words. He did not intermeddle in these men affairs but left them to perform the duties he had been commanded by God to appoint them to do. As also, the apostle in Acts 6 did unto the seven.

Considering the fact that no two deacon books agree on the same thing, let us rely on the word of God instead. We know that God is not the author of confusion, therefore, we can only surmise that the writers of these books aim is to mislead or gain some sort of dictatorship authority over God' people. A move Peter warns leaders against. *(1 Peter 5:23) feed the flock of God which is among you, taking the oversight thereof, not by constraint, but willingly; not for filthy lucre, but of a ready mind; neither as being Lords over God's heritage, but being examples to the flock.* The preacher will quickly tell you the deacon is a servant. This is true but what they fail to realize is that they are also servants. Minister means one who serves. Jesus was a servant king. Peter, Paul, Timothy, Silas, Jude, James, and all the apostles were servants. (1 Peter 1:1, Jude 1:11, James 1:1, Titus 1:1, Phil. 1:1) we're all servants serving one true and eternal head (Jesus Christ). None of us are Lords over God' heritage, not only are deacons and ministers servants of God, they are servants of their congregation also. Jesus said in *Mat. 20: 27-28, "And whosoever will be chief among you, let him be your servant: Even as the Son of man came not to be ministered unto, but to minister, (to serve) and to give his life a ransom for many."* Here Jesus states that he came to be a servant. He came down to earth as a servant and to teach us how to serve our fellow man. *"John 3: 4-5 Jesus rose from supper and laid aside His garments, took a towel and girded Himself. After that, he poured water into a basin and began to wash the Disciples feet, and to wipe them with the towel with which he was girded."* Does this mean that he was a deacon? No! Every time the word servant is mentioned in the scriptures does not mean the person was or is a deacon or deaconess. It simply means the person is or was someone who served in a capacity that helped or aided the growth of the church in some supported role as the aged widows. The means may have been through finance, food, teaching, lodging, care, or etc. the work load of the church must be shared in order for the spiritual growth of the church to increase; each governing body doing their assigned responsibility. *1 Tim. 1:2 I exhort therefore, that, first of all, supplications, prayers, intercessions and giving of thank, be made for all men; for kings, and for **all** that are in authority; that we may lead a quiet and peaceable life in all godliness and honesty.*

How long is a deacon appointed to serve? First of all deacons like bishops and pastors are appointed, their office is one of desire and selection. Over the years, it has been stated that deacons are appointed to office for life. Were they wrong? No! Each congregation had and has the right to appoint and remove their deacons, like the pastor, when they no longer serve the needs of the church or if they do something unfitting to the office. The bible does not place a limitation on how long a deacon can or should serve. It does, however, commend deacons who serve well and acknowledges their good standing and boldness in the faith. The ministers who are the writers of the various deacon books place a different time limit on how long they think a deacon should serve but since the deacon serves the congregation it is not the pastor's place to determine how long the deacon should serve. It is the congregation choice to choose and remove. By the way, each deacon's book I've read seems to have a different opinion concerning the number of years. One says two years; another says five years. Others have different opinions concerning the number of years a deacon should serve but these are opinions and only opinions not truths. Should they be allowed to serve for life? I believe that as long as a deacon or a pastor is an asset to the growth of the church in the office he holds he should be allowed to continue to serve in that office. Wisdom led by the Holy Spirit is essence for the guidance of the church. Remember the selection of the deacon and pastor warrant they be honest, respectable, trustworthy, dependable, equipped with the Holy Spirit, well likeable in Christian character, and able to manage their own home well.

Since the deacon' office is an appointed office of the church, (Phil. 1: 1) the Apostle Paul addresses him with respect. *Paul and Timothy, the servants of Jesus Christ, to all the saints in Christ Jesus which are at Philippi with the bishops and deacons;* in this salutation, Paul addresses co-workers of the faith not leaders and table servers. To be a co-worker with the bishop (pastor) one must also know the word of God. The scriptures say, *"Be ye doers of the word and not hearers only, deceiving yourselves." (James 1:22) (Roman 2:13)"For not the hearers of the law are just in the sight of God, but the doers of the law will be justified."* This is a true statement. No one can do or teach what he/she doesn't know. We can only teach what we know and testify to what we've seen. Too often we try to convert others before we're converted ourselves. Jesus told Peter to wait until he was converted then strengthen his brethren Luke 22:32. *If we know to do right and fail to do it we will be whip with many stripes. Excuses of not knowing will not free us from the stripes of the whip. The more we know or are expected to know the more will be required of us St. Luke 12:47.* Deacons, like pastors, are expected to know and do what the office requires whether they're qualified or not. Should preachers and deacons be held accountable for wrong doings? Yes! It is outlined in Mat. 18: 15-17 for all brethren and 1 Tim.19-20 for elders (preachers). If the church does not hold them accountable, the evil will grow worse and worse causing others to sin also. Leaders must be examples of good not evil. The pastor and deacon should be the first to uphold the rules of the church and the last to even consider breaking one. The church should never show respect of person in cases of wrong doings James 2:8-9. There is no respect of person with God according to Romans 2:11.

Let's look at some of the offices and administrations God has set (placed) in the church. Some will tell you that he only placed the preacher in the church but the scripture disagrees with that statement. In 1 Cor. 12: 27-30, we read. *"Now ye are the body of Christ, and members in particular. And God hath set some (the members) in the church, first apostles, secondarily prophets, (Preachers, elders) thirdly teachers, after that miracles, then gifts of healings, helps, governments, diversities of tongues. Are all apostles? Are all prophets? Are all teachers? Are all workers of miracles? Have all the gifts of healing? Do all speak in tongues? Do all interpret?* The first through the eleventh verse tell us of the differences of administrations and diversities of operations but the same lord and God is in and overall. Notice he also placed governments in the church. It was not the preachers that placed governments in the church but God. The deacon board serves as a governing body of the church. They're placed there to deal with the many conflicts and other disagreements that erupt in the church pertaining to this life. The bible does not support the theory of a single person dealing with the conflicts of the church. In every situation where problems arose they were settled by a delegate of elders or apostles and elders but never by a single person or pastor. Let's review a few scripture verses. The incident of Peter at Cornelius house

(Acts 11 chapter), Paul before James and the elders (Acts 21), Paul before the chief priests and all their council (Acts 22-23) Paul before Agrippa, Festus, Bernice, the chief captains and principal men of the city (Acts 25) Paul before the chief of the Jews at Rome (Acts 28) the twelve apostles with the multitude (Acts 6), Paul before the apostles, elders, and whole church at Jerusalem (Acts 15). When problems arise in the church, they should be settled by the church or a group acting as the representatives of the church. The church is defined as a group of baptized believers in Christ. One man is one person but it takes a group joined together in Jesus' name to be the church. The preacher is not the church being alone therefore he cannot solve the problems of the church alone but must have the guidance as well as the support of the body or deacon board.

Since there's no ordained delegate of apostles or elders in the church today, it stands to reasons that the board of deacon must fulfill the function once filled by the delegate of elders. As recorded in the scripture, all church disagreements were settled by a governing body of the church. In the Jerusalem church, the apostles was one governing body, the seven was appointed to be one, and the brethren that the apostles asked to choose the seven was one. It is only natural to assume that as other needs arose other groups were put in place and the scriptures are our guide. Let's learn to follow God' words and stop following the word of heresy. I urge every deacon to examine himself to choose whether he is qualified or not for the office he holds. To the pastors, I plead; learn to work together in harmony with the deacons. A divided church cannot stand. The building may remain but the hearts of the people will chock as long as divisions exist within the congregation or among the pastor and deacons. We should all remember that it was greed and the desire for power that caused Satan to be cast down.

The deacon board does not serve at the discretion of the pastors but of God. Governments were placed in the church at the approval of God Acts 6:7. It was only at God' approval that these men were filled with the Holy Ghost and Philip did not serve at the Apostles discretion but was commissioned by the spirit. (Exodus 18:23) (Acts, 8:26:39-40) The word of God increased because of the service of these seven men and we know only God can add to the church. In both passive of scriptures, we see peace and harmony was the result. It was not the Apostles idea but the Holy Spirit acting through them that made the suggestion to choose these men. *1 Peter 1:21 " For prophecy never came by the will of man but holy men of God spoke as they were moved by the holy spirit."* If a thing is not of God, it will not stand. The apostles in acts 6 spoke as they were directed by the Holy Spirit and the government appointed by them through the guidance of the Holy Spirit has stood down through the ages and have been a great influence to and for the growth and peace keeping harmony of the church. All good things are of God. If a thing is not of God it will not stand but if it be of God you cannot overthrow it Acts 5:38-39. The deaconship is a co-government of the church. Every level of government has its responsibility and each should work together to build and edify the church. We should always remember the words of Jesus in St. Mat.3:15 *"Suffer it to be so now: for thus it become us to fulfill all righteousness."* I pray that God will open up the minds of men and women to the truths of his word. To every fellow deacon, I urge you to search the scriptures, learn of them, follow them, and do your very best to live a life style that you and those you serve will be proud of. May God be with you and guide you in all truths.

Man's Opinions vs. God's Word

I call your attention now to a few of man' opinions verses God' words; you decide in your heart who you believe is right.

1. The highest court in our land declares it's right and legal for a man to marry a man and a woman to marry a woman. (a) God' word says a man shall leave his father and his mother and be joined to his wife and they shall become one flesh (Gen 2:24). God brought a woman to Adam not a man to be a help meet. A woman and a man can produce; a man and a man cannot. A woman and a woman cannot.

2. The man who holds the highest office in our land, the president of the United States, as well as most of our politicians, our courts, and a large number of church goers supports homosexuality as being right and just in the sight of God. They support gay marriages, gay pastors and other church leaders and have the belief that God made them that way. (A) God' words state that people who possess such character traits shall not enter the kingdom of heaven. *(1 Cor. 6:9) do you not know that the*

unrighteous will not inherit the kingdom of God? Do not be deceived, neither fornicators, nor idolaters, nor adulterers, nor homosexuals, (effeminates), nor sodomites, nor thieves, nor covetous, nor drunkards, nor revilers, nor extortionists will inherit the kingdom of God. And such were some of you but you were washed, but you were sanctified, but you were justified in the name of the Lord Jesus and by the spirit of our God. These verses reveal that a person can change and must change in order to inherit eternal life. Unless such a change is made, these individuals will not enter the kingdom. The sin of homosexuality was great in the cities of Sodom and Gomorrah. It was so bad that men preferred men over women (Gen. 19:4-8). The same trend seems to be growing strong in our lands today. We should take note of what God did to Sodom and Gomorrah and turn from this evil while we still have a change.

3. We have so many experts today who profess to know more about raising children than God our creator. God' word says, in Prov. 13:24, *he who spares his rod hates his son, but he who loves him disciplines him promptly. (Prov. 19:18) chasten thy son while there is hope and let*

not thy soul spare for his crying. Solomon, the wisest man that ever lived, instructs us through the guidance of the Holy Spirit to discipline our children while they're young and still under our control. If we love our children, we should train them while they're young to respect all that is good and right. He tells us not to be weary because of their tears. It is better we use the rod to teach them right and wrong while they're teachable than let them fall in the hands of this world' system for discipline. If we allow that to happen, we'll be the ones sharing the tears. (A) Our worldly experts say it's wrong to whip the child. They offer a milder means of punishment. They say things like sending them to their rooms and standing in a corner for a period of time is a more sufficient mean of punishment.

In the days of our fore parents, they used God' method for disciplining children and children grew up with respect for parents, God, and their fellow man. Consider where our children are today in means of respect. They're unruly, ungraceful, and disrespectable toward parents, teachers, and the law. Yet, we continue to follow the worldly Expert' advice and denies God' method and we have the nerves to ask what happen when our children go astray. (Prov. 22:15) *Foolishness is bound in the heart of a child; but the rod of correction shall drive it far from him.* Man has made many efforts to place his opinions above God' words. How long will we halt between God' word and man' opinions?

A final note: the qualifications for bishops (pastors) and deacons are somewhat similar both are required to be faithful, respectable, and honest to God and church. Bishops (Pastors) must understand the desire to be bishops (pastors) are strictly their choice 1 Tim.3:1. When they choose to do so, it is their personal confession to God stating their qualifications are in order according to the scriptures and that they (the pastors) accept the responsibility and honor of overseeing and feeding the flock of God or the penalty for neglect of duty. (Jer. 10:21) *For the shepherds (pastors) have become dull hearted, and have not sought the Lord; therefore they shall not prosper, and all their flocks shall be scattered. (Jer. 23:1) "Woe to the shepherds who destroy and scatter the sheep of my pasture!" says the Lord. Therefore thus says the Lord God of Israel against the shepherds (pastors) who feed my people;" you have scattered my flock, driven them away, and not attended to them. Behold, I will attend to you for the evil of your doings," says the Lord.* Those pastors that continue to rob God' flock of nourishment and spiritual guidance, God will truly punish them for their evil and neglect of duty.

For the deacon, it is not an office of personal desire but an office of need, search, appointment, and service (Acts 6:1-3). There should first be a need then a search for ones whose qualifications are in line with scriptures, selections should be made on the merits of their godly deeds and devotions. Next, they should be evaluated and tried until the congregation is absolutely sure of their worthiness. When this has been proven to the church' satisfaction, he/they shall be presented to the pastor for appointment to the office of the deaconship for service. (Acts.6:1-3) (1 Tim.3:10) if you'd notice in Acts 6:3, the selection should be made by the Brethren or church not the pastors. The Pastors job is to see the need and make the appointment. The church' job is to do the selection and approving. If the Congregation neglects to select men according to scriptural qualifications, the church will suffer the consequences. Then the blame game will start with everybody having an opinion. When will we ever learn that attending church services does not mean a person has been converted? However, if one has been converted and is saved, one will not hesitate to assemble with other believers.

Part 2

The Works of the Flesh

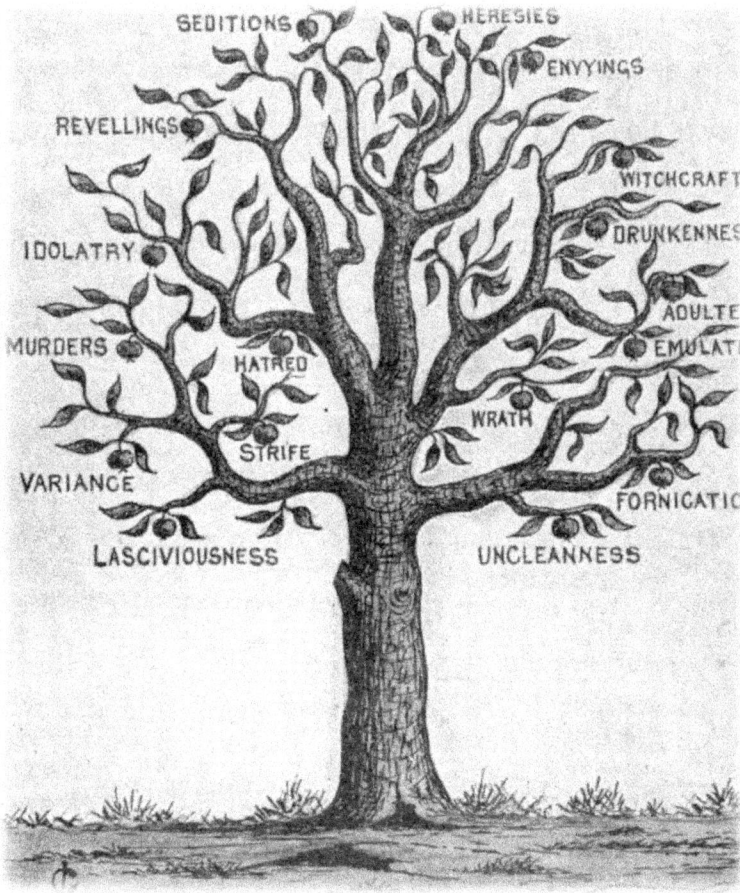

Introduction

The rivalry of flesh and spirit is a constant battle
that the mind is faced with each day. The perceiving pages

are written to introduce you to twenty-one works of the flesh and nine fruits of the spirit. There are many that you may not be aware of and you may not realize they can have a great bearing on your salvation. At least one of these things, if not more, at one point in time has been at work in each of our lives. Ecclesiastes tells us there's a time and season for everything. God allows each of us a certain amount of time on this earth. In that time, most of us will have the time to choose whether we're going to live a life dedicated to God or one dedicated to the love of the world. It is necessary for us to know that we or they who choose the way of the world cannot inherit the kingdom of God. Let's see what God's word says about the matter?

(Gal.5:19-21) *Now the works of the flesh are manifest* **(plain)** *which are these; adultery, fornication, uncleanness, lasciviousness, idolatry, witchcraft, hatred, variance, emulations, wrath, strife, seditions, heresies, envying, murders, drunkenness, revellings, and such like: of the which I tell you before, as I have also told you in time past, that they which do such things shall not inherit the kingdom of God.* Also, there're also others listed in 1 Cor.6:9-10. *Know ye not that the unrighteous shall not* *inherit the kingdom of God? Be not deceived: neither fornicators, nor idolaters, nor adulterers, nor effeminate, nor abusers of themselves with mankind, nor thieves, nor covetous, nor drunkards, nor revilers, nor extortioners, shall inherit the kingdom of God.* Don' let anyone deceive you with words telling you everything's alright because all have sinned and come short of the glory of God. In (1Cor.6:11), the apostle Paul writes concerning the Corinthian Christians and Christians of our day and time *"and such was some of you: but ye are washed, but ye are sanctified, but ye are justified in the name of the Lord Jesus, and by the Spirit of our God.* Here the apostle tells us that at some point in our lives we too engaged in one or more works of the flesh but once we found Jesus we put off the works of the flesh in order to receive salvation. Once we become saints the desire to engage in the works of the flesh should no longer appeal to us. (Eph. 5:3) *But fornication, and all uncleanness, or covetousness, let it not be ONCE named among you, as becometh saints.*

The works of the flesh are enticing luring fantasies of the devil. Once he gets a mind focused on the pleasures of the world, he knows that mind will be taken off of God and eternal life. Whether for a few seconds or for a few years, Satan takes pleasure in getting our minds focused on earthly pleasures. Just as he convinced Eve that she would not surely die for disobeying God, he has inspired many spiritual leaders to turn a deaf ear to the wrongs going on in their congregations. The true and living God hates evil and is not pleased with the disobedient of mankind that's on the rise today. His words say he made us male and female and that a man shall leave his father and mother and shall cleave unto his wife and they shall become one. The rib was taken out of man's side to make a woman as a help meet for man not for woman. God made every mammal to produce after their kind. It takes a male and female to produce; male and male, female and female cannot. Just because so many leaders are giving in to the devil wiles, it does not change God's word. God says the soul that sin, it shall die and that each of us will bear the penalty for our own iniquity (Ezek.18:20). Be sure you're on the road to salvation and not on the road to destruction.

Many of us can acknowledge that fornication has cut short a many dreams and destroyed a many careers.

The fornication one engages in in his/her early life sometime affects the rest of one's life. What was considered the norm was and is disobedient of God's word. The result of fornication has the ability to create life and the ability to destroy lives. Knowing or not knowing, that we sow we must also reap. The pleasures of disobedient weighted against righteousness always come up a failure.

The scriptures define a husband as the male of a marriage union and the woman as the female of the union. The Supreme Court's decision will now cause school books and dictionaries to be changed. According to their decision, a husband can no longer be defined as a male and a wife no longer as a female. Their decision gives men the rights to be called wives and women the rights to be called husbands. No longer will we be able to determine by sight who is considered the wife in a marriage or who is the husband. Millions of dollars will be spent to rewrite the world's definition of how to determine the husband from the wife in a relationship. God's definition has been plain and easy to determine for hundreds of years because

God is not the author of confusion but a God of truth and righteousness.

Too many, the things that are going on in the world today may seem unreal but they've been predicted by scriptures to come to pass. Though it seem new evils are been created every day, the world is just repeating itself. Ecclesiastes reminds us that *the things that have been, it **is that** which shall be; and that which is done **is** that which shall be done: and **there is** no new **thing** under the sun. That which hath been is now; and that which is to be hath already been; and God requireth that which is past (Eccl. 1:9 and 3:15).*

In Genesis chapter nine, we read where God said the imagination of man's heart **is** evil from his youth. In Proverbs twenty-two fifteen, Solomon tells us foolishness is bound in the heart of a child; but the rod of correction shall drive it far from him. Many of us can testify to this being true. When we were children, we know how the rod turned us from our evil deeds. If we're parents, we perhaps have experienced how sparing the rod has caused our own children to go astray. Satan is a resourceful being; he has no preference in the ones he uses. His favorite weapon is deceitfulness and if you resist him today he'll flee but he'll return back as early as tomorrow. Satan is not a human being therefore he bears no ill feelings toward resentments.

In these finally days, Satan is boldly spreading deceitfulness in the hearts of the believers. One of his most devastating acts was to take prayer out of the schools. Prayer is the way we communicate with God. The scriptures say men aught always pray and not faint. Children should be taught at a young age the value and necessity of prayer. Proverbs tells us we should train up a child in the way he should go: and when he is old, he will not depart from it (prov. 22:6). Children should be taught from a young age how and when to pray. As they grow older, they will encounter many situations where they'll need to call on the Lord. Therefore, they need to know when and how to pray. Many church people saw the act of taking prayer out of schools as no harm since children can be taught the necessity of prayer at church. What they fail to realize is that children are forced to go to school and would definitely be exposed to prayer but very few parents send or bring their children to church. Therefore, many will never get the chance to learn the value of prayer.

After getting prayer taken out of the schools as well as some government facilities, the atheists moved on to the next step of defying God's words by making it unlawful for parents to discipline their children without fear of punish. Discipline is a must in the rearing of children and throughout our adult lives. Without it, the world would become chaotic. Successfully getting this done, it gave the atheists more momentum for the next step.

The legalization of homosexuality, which scripture directs Christians to with stain from, is now being accepted by many church goers. The bible clearly states in 1 Cor. 6:9 that those who practice such things shall not inherit the kingdom of God yet many religious leaders are teaching their congregations that there's nothing wrong with being gay. They profess to be servants of God yet their words are the words of the devil. They blind people by the way they define God's relationship toward mankind. God is a God of love and mercy; this he has proven to us. God loves and will always love us all but not the sins we engage in. God loves all of his creation and does not wish any of us to be lost but we must heed his words, accept what it says, and be obedient to it. The wisest man that ever lived tells *us he that refuses instructions despises his own soul: but he that hears reproof gets understanding; cease, my son, to hear the instruction **that cause** to err from the words of knowledge (Prov.15:32 and **19:27**). For rebellion **is as** the sin of witchcraft, and stubbornness **is as** iniquity and idolatry (1 Samuel 15:23a).* Samuel also tells us to obey is better than sacrifice, **and** to hearken than the fat of rams (1 Samuel 15:22b). Finally, Romans 10 tells us faith and belief in Jesus Christ is essential for salvation, for he is the end of the law for righteousness, and only through him can we be saved. Jesus said in St. John 14:23 " if a man loves me, he will keep my words:' are we following and keeping The Lord' words or are we denying the Lord' words and following our nation' leaders and the men of the Supreme court words? Politicians and other leaders are bragging about being gay but they will have to someday stand before the Lord.

Adultery

Adultery- The seventh commandment, thou shalt not commit adultery. Adultery, under Hebrew law, covered the crime of unchaste, wherein a man, married or single, had illicit intercourse with a married or betrothed woman, not his wife. It was punishable by fire or stoning. Adultery also covers the sin of one being unfaithful to God by yielding to idols, sexual desires, or other worldly desires or things contrary to God's will or words. It was used figurative of friendship with the world in James 4:4. *Ye adulterers, and adulteresses, know ye not that the friendship of the world is enmity with God? Whosoever therefore will be a friend of the world is the enemy of God.* By looking upon a man or woman to lust after them, one commits adultery within the heart (Mat. 5:28). David committed such a sin with Bathsheba in 2 Sam. 11. The sin of adultery causes one to sink deeper and deeper into sin with an attempt to cover up the adulterous act. Notice how David tried to cover up his mistake with deception. When that didn't work, he resorted to murder. Lust caused David to break the tenth commandment; greed led him to break the seventh commandment; fear led him to resort to committing the sixth commandment. Committing these sins, David displeased God and reaped the punishment for disobedient the rest of his days. We can see through the example of David that the sin of adultery destroys homes and lives too.

Adultery can make one poor while increasing one's sin. (Prov.29:3) *Whoso loveth wisdom rejoiceth his father; but he that keepeth company with a harlot spendeth **his** substance. (Prov.6:26) For by means of a whorish woman **a man is brought** to a piece of bread: and the adulteress will hunt for the precious life. (Prov.23:27-28) "For a whore **is** a deep ditch; and a strange woman **is** a narrow pit. She also lieth in wait as **for** a prey, and increaseth the transgressors among men."*

There are many good men and women today living in adultery by marriage and are not aware of it. Listen to what Paul says about the matter. (Rom.7:2-3) *For the woman which hath a husband is bound by the law to **her** husband so long as he liveth; but if the husband be dead, she is loosed from the law of **her** husband. So then if, while **her** husband liveth, she be married to another man, she* *shall be called an adulteress: but if her husband be dead, she is free from that law; so that she is no adulteress, though she be marred to another man.* God only justifies divorce on the grounds of fornication. If divorce is granted on any others ground, the end thereof could be adultery. (Mat.5:31-32) *It hath been said, whosoever shall put away his wife, let him give her a writing of divorcement: but I say unto you, that whosoever shall put away his wife, saving for the cause of fornication, causeth her to commit adultery: and whosoever shall marry her that is divorced committeth adultery.*

From the beginning of the nation of Israel, God placed strict rules in place to guard against adultery among them. (Lev.20:10) *"And the man that committeth adultery with **another** man's wife, **even he** that committeth adultery with his neighbor's wife, the adulterer and the adulteress shall surely be put to death."* If God's law was physically being punished today, there would be large lines of ministers, deacons, politicians, judges, and people from all walks of life lined up to be stoned. Grace gives us an opportunity to stop the act and get our lives back in order before physical death claims us and condemns us to a lost stage.

Then there is that spiritual adultery committed by church goers. They pretend to serve God yet they obey not his word. We commit adultery against God when we as Christians put other gods before the all living eternal God. Gods like our jobs, cars, money, houses, education, and even our complexion and looks. Remember it was Satan's beauty that corrupted his wisdom causing him to be uplifted with pride (Eze.28:12, 17). Beauty was also presence in the mind of Eve when she took of the forbidden fruit (Gen.3:6). It was also beauty that attracted David to Bathsheba (2 Sam.11:2). Beautiful women brought Solomon, the wisest man that ever lived, down. Beauty brought the strongest man, Samson, to his shame and beauty today turns many men and women from the faith. Adultery is a powerful lust of the flesh but one we can overcome with the help of the Lord Jesus Christ.

(Prov.6:32) **But** *whoso committeth adultery with a woman lacketh understanding:* **he that** *doeth it destroyeth his own soul.* If King David had only known that

committing adultery would cause his life to be shaken, he would have thought twice before desiring to sleep with another man's wife. One night of pleasure with a beautiful woman caused him to regret it the rest of his life. He saw his act of unfaithfulness played out through his children. Through witnessing the rape, adultery, and murder, his children committed, he not only saw but witnessed the hurt that he had placed upon his family, the family of Uriah, and the disappointment of God and his servants who were forced to partake in his actions.

The impact of our actions is fully felt after they're acknowledged by us and are known by others. Samson never thought telling the secret of his great strength to Delilah would cause him to be captured by his enemies. When others know our weaknesses and faults, we become vulnerable to their powers. They gain a persuasive power over our lives.

Heb. 13:4 declares *marriage to be honorable in all, and the bed undefiled: but whoremongers and adulterers God will judge.* As the proprietor of an honest dollar is more respectable than the proprietor of a dishonest dollar, it is more honorable to marry than to associate with whores and whoremongers. Association with the ungodly can only bring a good man or woman down in character and influence. By avoiding adultery, we keep our good name and the respect of God and mankind. Knowing adultery can cause us to be lost, it is wise to avoid it at all cost.

Fornication

Fornication is a sin similar to adultery but it primarily deals with unchaste sex. It is a crime **(sin)** of impurity between unmarried persons. It is a sin that can cost one his/her entry into the kingdom of heaven. (1 Cor. 6:9) *know ye not that the unrighteous shall not inherit the kingdom of God? Don't be deceived neither fornicators, nor idolaters …. Shall inherit the kingdom of God;* this verse tells us that if we're engaged in sexual activity outside of marriage then we're in danger of hell's fire. Church goers deceive themselves thinking that God does not require them to live righteously. They hide behind the saying in Roman 3:23 *"For all have sinned, and come short of the glory of God.* This verse tells us that none of us can or have lived up to what God created us to be but it does not give us a license to sin. It in simple terms tells us that because of our weaknesses we must rely on Jesus in order to be saved. We cannot live a righteous enough life to save ourselves because our flesh is too weak. (Roman 6:1) *What shall we say then? Shall we continue in sin that grace may abound? Certainly not! How shall we who died to sin live any longer in it?* Fornication, which is a grave sin, can and will cause you to be lost. (Roman 6:23) *"For the wages (payment) of sin is death, but the gift of God is eternal life in Christ Jesus our Lord."*

In this day and time, many consider fornication a way of life. Many young girls think their bodies are money making machines while young boys think having sex with multiple partners is a sign of real man hood. This may mainly be because they've not been taught about the seriousness of the sin of fornication. So few people today read their bibles and many of those who do fail to get an understanding of what they're reading. Ministers and pastors sway away from rebuking members who've done wrong. Partly because many of them are living in sin; it is not uncommon to see ministers with multiple wives yet the scripture says a bishop must be the husband of one living wife. (1 Tim. 3:2) Another reason, may be because many sinners are the biggest money payers among the church congregation and the pastors don't want to upset the flow of money coming into the treasury. They fail to see that the church was not set up to save money but to save souls. God is able and have always been able to inspire in the hearts of his people to give enough money to support the needs of the church. They may not pay enough to support the worldly activities that have become a part of our churches but certainly enough to pay all bills and other necessary obligations of the church. Yet, a third and sadder reason, maybe they simply do not know the word of God.

One of the most disturbing things today is to see leaders of churches uplifting unwed mothers in their fornication by parading their offspring in the church. They should never condemn the mother, father, or child but they should let them know that fornication is wrong in the sight of God. Supporting their sin rather than denouncing it, they have forgotten their charge. (2 Tim. 4:1-2) *I charge you therefore before God and the Lord, Jesus Christ, who will judge the living and the dead at his appearing and his kingdom: Preach the word! Be ready in season and out of season. Convince, rebuke, exhort, with all long suffering and teaching.* To keep from hurting anyone' feeling, they keep their mouth closed turning a deaf ear to the wrong. (Proverbs 27:5) *Open rebuke is better than love carefully concealed.* Wrong is wrong no matter who does it. Fornication is wrong in the sight of man and God whether it's done by the preacher, the deacon, lay person, or any unwed man, woman, boy, or girl and it is parents and church leader's responsibility to say so. It is the responsibility of preachers to warn their congregation about the effects of fornication and all others sins. Ezekiel 3:17-21 *Son of man, I have made thee a watchman unto the house of Israel: therefore hear the word at my mouth, and give them warning from me. When I say unto the wicked, thou shalt surely die; and thou give him not warning, nor speak to warn the wicked from his wicked way, to save his life; the same wicked man shall die in his iniquity; but his blood will I require at your hand. Yet, if thou warn the wicked and he turn not from his wickedness, nor from his wicked way, he shall die in his iniquity; but thou hast delivered thou soul. Again, when a righteous man doth turn from his righteousness, and commit iniquity, and I lay a stumbling block before him, he shall die: because thou hast not given him warning, he shall die in his sin, and his righteousness which he hath done shall not be remembered; but his blood will I require at thine hand. Nevertheless if thou warn the righteous man, that the righteous sin not, and he doth not sin, he shall surely live, because he is warned; also thou hast delivered thy soul.* Leaders are held responsible for what they teach and what they do not teach their congregation about the cost of sin.

Fornication is a wrecker of homes and the body. When a woman or man commits fornication it causes a break down in their relationship or in their marriage whichever the case may be. When a man commits fornication with another woman and a child is involved, he has a secret that he has to hide as well as an expense. Eventually, money problems will arise causing an upset to the marriage relationship. On the other hand, when a woman gets involved with another man and get with a child, she has to lie to the husband and the child to hide her unfaithfulness. Because of fornication and adultery, many children grow up never knowing who their real father is. The woman also has to live with the fear of her unchaste relationship becoming known. It is a true fact that if more than one person knows your secret then one too many people knows. One person cannot commit fornication on his or her own. It takes at least two people. How trustworthy is your indulging partner? The news of fornication spreads like the news spoken concerning the king. (*Ecclesiastes 10:20*) *Curse not the king, no not in thy*

thought; and curse not the rich in thy bedchamber: for a
bird of the air shall carry the voice, and that which hath
wings shall tell the matter. Don't fool yourself; if you've
committed the act, somebody knows about it. People who
want tell their secrets loves telling yours. Let's consider
fornication and the harm to the body. In every major city,
a vast population is infected with some sort of venereal
disease caused by fornication or adultery. Today among
the hip generation, fornication is the hike of life. We worry
about sending our children to school because teachers and
other instructors take advantage of them. We worry about
sending our children to camps because camp leaders take
advantage of them. Our police officers take advantage, our
sport directors take advantage, relatives take advantage
and today more and more ministers are becoming sexually
involved with the youths of their church. It seems we're
living in a sexual generation where venereal diseases,
righteousness, respect, and honor, mean nothing.

(1Cor.6:13b, 18) *"Now the body is not for*
fornication, but for the Lord; and the Lord for the body.
Flee fornication. Every sin that a man doeth is without the
body; but he that commits fornication sin against his own
body. What? Know ye not that your body is the temple of

the Holy Ghost which is in you, which ye have of God, and ye are not your own. Fornication not only destroys the physical body it also destroys the spiritual body. Paul says it is best for a man not to even touch a woman but if he doesn't have the strength to resist then let him marry and make it sacred. (1 Cor. 7:9) *But if they cannot contain, let them marry: for it is better to marry than to burn.* Some people will tell you they don't want to be burdened down with a partner when they can have diver partners. This way of thinking may seem like fun on this side of the grave but if you die in your fornication you will be lost on the other side of the grave. Having a few years of fun, is it worth eternity in hell?

There was a time when mothers taught their daughters to save themselves for marriage. That is no longer a thing that's being taught. Even church going mothers encourage their daughters to try diver partners before thinking of getting married. Unaware they're teaching their children to sin against God's commandment. Christian parents should teach their children to obey God's commandments but they themselves should be examples of the things they teach.

Just because everybody seems to be engaging in the act don't make it right nor will it keep them from suffering because of the act. Fornication is not only a sin that can cause one to be lost; it is also one that can ruin one's life.

Fornication is such a harsh sin; it is the only sin that can justify divorcing a wife in the sight of God (Mat.5:31-32). Paul said *it is good for a man not to touch a woman. Nevertheless, **to avoid** fornication, let every man have his own wife, and let every woman have her own husband (1Cor.7:1b-2). But fornication, and all uncleanness, or covetousness, let it not be once named among you, as become saints (Eph.5:3).*

Fornication is a wide open sin today and few people seem to realize its impact on the family, the church, the community, or the off springs brought into this world by means of fornication. People are quick to recognize shacking as a means of living in fornication but they fail to realize that any woman or man who sells their body for money or profit is also guilty of fornication. The prostitute who parades up and down the streets knows he/she is committing fornication and knows it's wrong but the woman or man who secretly engages in illicit sex fail to realize their wrong. Whether they're doing it in the open or behind closed doors, it's still fornication and according to scripture, no fornicator shall inherit the kingdom of God.

*Seek ye the Lord while he may be found, call ye upon him while he is near: let the wicked forsake his way, and the unrighteous man his thoughts: and let him return to the Lord, and he will have mercy upon him; and to our God, for he will abundantly pardon. For as the rain cometh down, and the snow from heaven, and returneth not thither, but watereth the earth, and maketh it bring forth and bud, that it may give seed to the sower, and bread to the eater: So shall my word be that goeth forth out of my mouth: it shall not return unto me void, but it shall accomplish that which I please, and it shall prosper **in the thing** whereto I sent it (Is.55:6-7 and 10-11).* Hebrew 6:18 says it's impossible for God to lie. The unrighteous must change his/her ways if he/she want to inherit the kingdom of God and Christ.

The recent decision of the Supreme Court has sparked a height in the future of fornication and adultery. Now the law of the land, which is against God's word, makes it legal for a man to have sex with a man and a woman to have sex with a woman. As man continue to denounce God's word, it brings the wrath of God down upon this world. The many disasters appearing around the world are the beginning of sorrows (Mat 24). The more we give in to sin the more sorrows we'll have to face.

Uncleanliness

Uncleanliness is that which is polluted or defiled: polluted means to defile; defile means to make the pure impure. Impure means ritually unclean; mixed with foreign elements: no unclean person shall have inheritance in the kingdom of Christ and of God. (Eph.5:5) *For God has not called us to uncleanness but unto holiness. (1Thes.4:7) Wherefore come out from among them, and be ye separate, saith the Lord and touch not the unclean thing; and I will receive you.(2Cor.6:17)* in Mat.15:18-20, Jesus tells us the things that defiles a man. All these things originate and come forth out of the heart. These are things that make us impure.

In Lev.11:44, the Israelites were warned not to defile themselves with any creeping thing that creeps upon the earth. Man and woman are forbidden to lie down with a beast. (Lev.18:23) *Cursed **be** he that lie with any manner of beast. (Deut.27:21a)* The 15th chapter tells us when a person is found to be unclean, things and persons that come in contact or associates with him/her will be looked upon as being unclean. Paul tells us to separate ourselves from any man that is called a brother of the church who is involved in things that makes him unclean according to the faith. (1 Cor.5:11) *Also thou shalt not approach unto a woman to uncover her nakedness, as long as she is put apart for her uncleanness (lev.18:19).* It is uncleanness to lie with a woman during her menstrual period.

*When a man hath taken a wife, and married her, and it comes to pass that she find no favor in his eyes, because he hath found some uncleanness in her: then let him write her a bill of divorcement, and give **it** in her hand, and send her out of his house (Deut.24:1).* Unfaithfulness can cause one to be unclean in a relationship whether the relationship is between a man and woman or between mankind and God. Anyone who takes pleasure in and is involved in the works of the flesh is considered unclean to preach the gospel. As it is impossible for the blind to lead the blind, lest both fall into the ditch, it is also impractical for the unclean to gain confident or support to lead the clean. 1Peter1:15—16 say, *"But as he, which hath called you, is holy, so be ye holy in all manner of conversation; because it is written, be ye holy; for I am holy."* Finally, Paul tells us in 1Cor.7:1, *having therefore these promises,* *dearly beloved, let us cleanse ourselves from all filthiness of the flesh and spirit, perfecting holiness in the fear of God."*

Lasciviousness

Lasciviousness is defined as unbridled lust. An uncontrollable sexual or luxuriant desire for wantonness without regard for what is right. It begins and flow from the heart. (Mark 7:21-23) *For from within, out of the heart of men, proceed evil thoughts, adulteries, fornications, murders, thefts, covetousness, wickedness, deceit, lasciviousness, an evil eye, blasphemy, pride, foolishness: all these evil things come from within, and defile the man.*

In 1 Peter 4:1a-3 it characterizes the old life in us. *For he that hath suffered in the flesh hath ceased from sin; that he no longer should live the rest of his time in the flesh to the lusts of men, but to the will of God. For the time past of our life may suffice us to have wrought the will of the Gentiles, when we walked in lasciviousness,* **(lewdness)** *lusts,* **(coveting things in an evil manner or unlawful)** *excess of wine,* **(drunkenness)** *revellings,* **(revelries)** *banquetings,* **(drinking parties)** *and abominable idolatries.* Here the apostle tells us we have spent enough of our past life serving the will of our flesh, now, since we've been converted, we should serve the will of God and our Lord Jesus Christ.

Jude 1:4 describes lasciviousness as a sign of apostasy. **(An abandoning of the faith)** *"For there are certain men crept in unawares, who were before of old ordained to this condemnation, ungodly men, turning the grace of our God into lasciviousness, and denying the only Lord God, and our Lord Jesus Christ.* Paul found this sin among the church at Corinth. ***And*** *lest, when I come again, my God will humble me among you, and* ***that*** *I shall bewail* ***(mourn)*** *many which have sinned already, and have not repented of the uncleanness, and fornication and lasciviousness which they have committed.* Lasciviousness is an indecent and obscene sin that can rob a person's chance of entering the kingdom of God. (Gal.5:19)

The men of Sodom and Gomorrah had a burning desire for men over women (Genesis 19). This wicked desire and practice of their' eventually brought down fire and brimstone upon them from the Lord and destroyed them. In Romans chapter 1, Paul tells us that men's wickedness will again grow to that point. All around us today, we see and hear of men having a burning desire for other men and women having a burning desire for other women. It seems, our world is returning to the ways of Sodom and Gomorrah and God will not close his eyes to such evil.

Idolatry

Idolatry is the worship of idols. Idols are things we worship other than God. The worship of idols has been around for many years. In Genesis chapter 31, when Rachel stole her father's idols, it caused Laban to pursue after Jacob with anger in his heart. In those days, people believed strongly in their idol gods. They worshiped many strange and different gods. The national god of the Philistines was Dagon Judges 16: 21-23. It was this Dagon that fell before the ark of God at Ashdod. (1 Sam 5:1-5) and eventually all false gods will perish before the true and living God and the Lord Jesus Christ.

Man in ancient time worshipped things made of stone, wood, clay, and even vines. They had their sun god, moon god, fertility god, fire god, love god, river god, and a god for just about every other walk of life. The Living God, Jehovah, forbade the Israelites from worshiping any other god. The first of his commandments for them to follow is recorded in Exodus 20:3-6. *Thou shalt have no other gods before me. Thou shalt not make unto thee any graven image, or any likeness **of anything** that **is** in heaven above,* *or that **is** in the earth beneath, or that **is** in the waters under the earth: thou shalt not bow down thyself to them, nor serve them: for I the Lord thy God **am** a jealous God, visiting the iniquity of the fathers upon the children unto the third and fourth **generation** of them that hate me; and showing mercy unto thousands of them that love me, and keep my commandments.*

We, the church, are the spiritual children of Abraham through Jesus Christ. That means, since we're God' people, we are still bound by these commandments. The people in ancient time were primitive, unlearned, and superstitious, yet they were punished for their disobedient. Peter says in 1 Peter 4: 17-18 *"for the time **is** come that judgment must begin at the house of God: **(the church, the place people know the word of God but refuse to live or teach it)** and if **it** first **begin** at us, **(the church)** what shall the end **be** of them that obey not the gospel of God? And if the righteous scarcely be saved, where shall the ungodly and sinner appear?* Our Leaders ignorant and playful altitudes and excuses will not protect them when they're ordered to appear before Christ at the judgment. St. Luke says, "We who know to do right shall be whip with many stripes." To know the word of God and turn from it or deliberately disobey it is a dangerous thing. Peter says, *"For it had been better for them not to have known the way of righteousness, than, after they have known **it,** to turn from the holy commandment delivered unto them." (2peter2:21)*

Many leaders allow gays, adulterers, adulteress, bigamists, drunkards, fornicators, and other sinners in their pulpits. Out of pride and friendship, they allow these people to serve but refuse to tell them they're undesirable candidates for the gospel according to God' word; they know what Gal. 5:19 says but for some reason they ignore God' word not realizing they're serving Satan and denying God. That is idolatry.

1Timothy 3: 1. Says the bishop must be blameless. Gal. 5: 19-21 lists the works of the flesh. Anyone who falls in either of these categories cannot enter the kingdom of heaven and they should be told. When leaders fail to tell people of their wrongs and the one who does wrong dies in his/her sin, the leader will bear a part of that person' sin. This is why James say, (James 3:1- 2) *my brethren, be not many masters, knowing that we shall receive the greater condemnation. For in many things we offend all. If* any man offend not in word the same *is* a perfect man, *and* able also to bridle the whole body. We all have an obligation to serve God. To serve self, friendship, fear, pride, or the likes, is idolatry. (Eph.5:5-6) *For this ye know, that no whoremonger, nor unclean person, nor covetous man, who is an idolater, hath any inheritance in the kingdom of Christ and God. Let no man deceive you with vain (conceited) words:*

for because of these things cometh the wrath of God upon the children of disobedience.

As Christians, we're warned against idol worshipping. Idol worship is demonical. *What say I then? That the idol is anything, or that which is offered in sacrifice to idols is anything? But, I say, that the things which the Gentiles sacrifice, they sacrifice to devils, and not to God: and I would not that ye should have fellowship with devils. Ye cannot drink the cup of the Lord, and the cup of devils: ye cannot be partakers of the Lord' table, and of the table of devils (1Cor.10:19-21).*

It is irrational for Christians to serve idols. Acts 17:29 says *"forasmuch then as we are the offspring of God, we ought not to think that the Godhead is like unto gold,* or silver, or stone, graven by art and man's device." The apostle, John, in 1John tell Christians to keep away from idols and Paul follows up by telling Christians to not keep company with a brother that is an idolater (1Cor.5:11). As Christians, we serve the living and true God. Idol gods should have no place in our lives.

Witchcraft

Witchcraft is defined as the working of black magic. It is a form of sorcery practiced by sorcerers and witches. It was forbidden in Israel. (Deut. 18:9-14) *When thou art come into the land which the Lord thy God give thee, thou shalt not learn to do after the abominations of those nations. There shall not be found among you **any one** that make his son or his daughter to pass through the fire, **or** that use divination, **or** an observer of times, or an enchanter, or a witch, or a charmer, or a consulter with familiar spirits, or a wizard, or a necromancer. For all that do these things **are** an abomination unto the Lord: and because of these abominations the Lord thy God doth drive them out from before thee. Thou shalt be perfect with the*

Lord thy God. For these nations, which thou shalt possess, hearkened unto observers of times, and unto diviners but as for thee, the Lord thy God hath not suffered thee so **to do.**

In 1 Sam.28:1-14, we read where King Saul had put those that had familiar spirits and the wizards out of the land but after the death of Samuel we see Saul seeking the service of a woman with a familiar spirit. Because of his sin, the Lord had departed away from him and Samuel was dead so he had no one to advise him how to face the conflict with the Philistines.

In Micah 5:12-14a, the Lord through the prophet condemned witchcraft. *And I will cut off witchcraft out of thine hand; and thou shalt have no* **more** *soothsayers: thy graven images also will I cut off, and thy standing images out of the midst of thee; and thou shalt no more worship the work of thine hands. And I will pluck up thy groves out of the midst of thee:*

Witchcraft is a means of divination. Divination is the attempt to foretell the unknown by occult means. Paul and Silas encountered a woman with a spirit of divination who followed them until Paul became grieved and commanded the spirit in the name of Jesus Christ to come out of her. In Acts 13:6-11, Paul and Barnabas came face to face with a sorcerer that withstood them seeking to turn the deputy, Sergius Paulus, from the faith but he was unsuccessful and was struck with blindness for a season.

Witchcraft and all manner of divinations are subject to the power of God. As God' children, we have no need of black magic. We have only to ask and God will supply our needs.

Hatred

Hatred- to dislike something or someone with strong feelings, It's a feeling of a person who hates with intense dislike, aversion, or hostility;

Since hatred can cause a person to be lost, we are warned to watch our anger. Anger, if not dealt with, can grow into jealousy, hatred, and eventually murder. (Eph. 4:26) *be ye angry, and sin not: let not the sun go down upon your wrath:* if we should die in our anger, we die in our hatred which means we cannot enter the kingdom of heaven. Sometimes people hate others for no apparent reasons at all yet others have countless reasons why they hate. In Gen. 37:4-5, a father, by showing favoritism, caused his older sons to hate their brother. 2 Sam. 13:15-22 shows us an incident where rape caused one brother to hate the other eventually ending in murder. (Mat. 5:22a) *But I say to you that whoever is angry with his brother without a cause shall be in danger of the judgment.* We are admonished to love our enemies and do good to those that hate us. (Luke 6:27)

It has been said that there's a little bit of hate in all of us. The right amount of anger will bring it out but that doesn't mean we have an evil nature like some. (John 3:20) *For everyone that doeth evil hate the light neither cometh to the light, lest his deeds should be reproved.* Hypocrites love the darkness because their deeds are evil. They serve the deeds of darkness while pretending to be children of the light. Many people say they love the Lord but their neighbors they hate. (1John 4:20) *if a man say, I love God, and hate his brother, he is a liar: for he that love not his brother whom he hath seen, how can he love God whom he hath not seen?* Hatred is a sin that can cost one his/her salvation. We're warned to replace hatred with love. Love endures all things. The kingdom of heaven is a kingdom of love where no hate or haters can enter.

(Prov.8:13) *"The fear of the Lord **is** to hate evil: pride, and arrogance, and the evil way, and the forward mouth, do I hate.* We may hate evil things and evil ways but not evil people. No matter how mean or evil a person is, we should search and pray for a way to love the individual but hate the evil he/she does.

In June 2015, a young white man went into a black church while they were having bible class and pulled out a gun and shot twelve members of the congregation killing nine and wounding three. His stated reason was that he was trying to start a race war. Such an act, if successful, he believed would result in the loss of many lives. Many black and white people were stunned by this act yet others felt no remorse. Such a degree of hatred opened up the world's eyes to the fact that prejudice is still alive in America. This young man's heart was filled with hatred. This hatred, no doubt, was taught him from the age of a child by some adult. It is one thing to murder an individual but to go into a place where people are assembled to worship God takes a misguided or totally evil person. *Yea and all that will live godly in Christ Jesus shall suffer persecution. But evil men and seducers shall wax worse and worse, deceiving, and being deceived (2 Tim. 3:12-13).* For years, we've seen the rise of black on black crimes but it was only recent that we began to see the hidden ever growing continue white on black crimes. This was only made possible by the use of cell phones and other electronic equipment. Things that have been going on for years have finally came to the light. The prophecy of God is being fulfilled every day of our lives. We have only to look around; the evident stands out like a sore thumb.

Variance

Variance is a difference that produces controversy; state of discord or disagreement. To excite one against another by contention, rivalry, or verbal dispute: In Mat.10:35 Jesus said, *for I am come to set a man at variance against his father, and the daughter against her mother, and the daughter-in-law against her mother-in-law. And a man's foes **shall be** they of his own household.*

We see the difference between families unfolding in our world every day. Fathers are killing their infants and adult children; children are killing their parents; siblings are killing one another; disagreements are driving families to destroy themselves. Churches are falling apart from within because of disagreements. Nations are finding it hard to gain the support of their own people. Variance is spreading like a pledge in homes, communities, cities, states, churches, and nations alike.

Emulations

Emulations are the efforts or desires to equal or excel others. Jealous rivalry: to stir up, to excite movement to a certain point. (Rom. 11:14) *if by any means I may provoke to emulation* **them which are** *my flesh, and might save some of them:* Paul had a desire for Israel to be saved. (1 Cor.9:22) *to the weak became I as weak, that I might gain the weak: I am made all things to all* **men,** *that I might by all means save some. (1 Cor. 10:33) even as I please all* **men** *in all* **things,** *not seeking mine own profit, but the* **profit** *of many, that they may be saved.*

Emulation when used in a good sense thrives to encourage others to better themselves. It thrives to help others realize their potentials. We emulate our children to become respectable and honorable citizens. We emulate church members to become faithful followers of Jesus Christ. We emulate our own minds to be all that we can be. When used in an evil sense, it may degenerate into jealousy causing hatred for the good it sees in others. Some people hate others because of their possessions, knowledge and money, favorable appearance in the sight of others, and basically any and everything God has blessed them with. Our God is not only a mighty God; he's a rich and blessing God. What he blesses others with in life, he'll bless us with too. If we do well, as he told Cain, (Gen.4:7) we can look forward to God acceptance and blessings.

To emulate the accomplishments of others in a godly manner is honorable but be careful what you wish for. With accomplishments come responsibilities. Of whom much is given, much is required (Luke 12:48). The urge to keep up with the Jones has a tendency of causing many worries and sleepless nights.

Wrath

Wrath is violent anger; indignation; rage, any action carried out in great anger for punishment or vengeance. Roman 12:18-19 urges Christians to live peaceably with all men and reframe from avenging themselves for the Lord declares that vengeance belongs to him and he will repay those who mistreat or do his children wrong. The wrath of God is said to be great in Zech.7:2. Roman 9:22 say it's predestined. *He that believeth on the Son hath everlasting life: and he that believeth not on the Son shall not see life; but the wrath of God abideth on him. (John3:36)* One of the effects of God's wrath is seen in the great plague in Num.11:33. *And while the flesh **was** yet between their teeth, ere it was chewed, the wrath of the Lord was kindled against the people, and the Lord smote the people with a very great plague.* In Num14:20-35, it was kindled against Israel because of their disobedience which caused them to wander in the wilderness for forty years. As a result of his wrath, Israel was led into captivity (2 Chr.36:16-17). We human beings bring god's wrath upon us in many ways. In josh.22:20, it was brought on by sin. *Did not Achan the son* *of Zerah commit a trespass in the accursed thing, and wrath fell on all the congregation of Israel? And that man perished not alone in his iniquity.* One man's sin can cause God's wrath to fall upon many. More so, if the man is in a leadership position. If he holds an office among the body of Christ, and continues in his sin, the whole congregation will eventually suffer.

Another weakness of church people that brings on God's wrath is their fellowship with evil. *And Jehu the son of Hanani the seer went out to meet him, and said to king Jehoshaphat, shouldest thou help the ungodly, and love them that hate the Lord? Therefore is wrath upon thee from before the Lord.(1Chr.19:2)* Many church people and church leaders place ungodly people in leadership roles and go alone with their unfaithfulness for so called "peace sake." They place the friendship or fear of man over the righteousness of God. To them, it's more importance to look good in the sight of man than to be obedient in the sight of God. They fail to realize that giving in to ungodliness bring the wrath of God down upon the remnant of mankind.

Probably one of the greatest hypocritical excuses of people is their sympathy with evil. We must be strong and encourage others not to be taken in by evil through sympathy. Observe what Moses said to his brother, Aaron and his Sons. *And Moses said unto Aaron and unto Eleazar and unto Ithamar, his Sons, uncover not your heads, neither rend your clothes; lest ye die, and lest wrath come upon all the people: but let your brethren, the whole house of Israel, bewail the burning which the Lord hath kindled (Lev.10:6).* How often have we seen church people in positions whose sins are known by the whole congregation? Not wanting to hurt their feeling, we allow them to continue in their evil. We show sympathy for them in their wrong and allow them to continue to be a slander to the church. We would love to see them removed; we know they should be removed but we want God or someone else to do it.

We have deliverance from God's wrath through Christ. *But God commendeth his love toward us, in that, while we were yet sinners, Christ died for us. Much more then, being now justified by his blood, we shall be saved from wrath through him. (Rom.5:8-9)* In ancient times, Israel was given deliverance through atonement (Num.16:45-48). Humbleness is also a way to detour God's wrath. *Notwithstanding Hezekiah humbled himself for the* pride of his heart, **both** he and the inhabitants of Jerusalem, so that the wrath of the Lord came not upon them in the days of Hezekiah (2Chr.32:26).

The wrath of man toward man can also be devastating. False accusations against a person often cause anger and wrath. *And Jacob was wroth and chode with Laban: and Jacob answered and said to Laban, what **is** my trespass? What **is** my sin that thou hast so hotly pursued after me? (Gen.31:36)* Jealousy is another cause of wrath between human beings. *And Saul was very wroth, and the saying displeased him; and he said, they have ascribed unto David ten thousands, and to me, they have ascribed **but** thousands; and **what** can he have more but the kingdom? (1Sam.18:8)* The lack of respect may also cause wrath. *And when Haman saw that Mordecai bowed not, nor did him reverence, then was Ha'-man full of wrath (Esth.3:5).*

The effects of men wrath can be seen through their punishment. *A man of great wrath shall suffer punishment: for if you deliver **him**, yet thou must do it again (Prov.19:19).* Job says in Job 5:2, "For wrath killeth the foolish man, and envy slayeth the silly one."

Mob actions often kindles wrath. *And when they heard **these sayings** they were full of wrath and cried out, saying, great **is** Diana of the Ephesians. And the whole city was filled with confusion: and having caught Gaius and Aristarchus, men of Macedonia, Paul's companions in travel, they rushed with one accord into the theater (Acts 19:28-29).*

There are also ways we can pacify or soften wrath. *A soft answer turn away wrath: but grievous words* stir up anger (prov.15:1). It takes at least two to argue. It is hard for wrath to continue when confronted with kindly suggestions or love. Consider the case of Naaman. *And Elisha sent a messenger unto him, saying, go and wash in Jordan seven times, and thy flesh shall come again to thee, and thou shalt be clean. But Naaman was wroth, and went away, and said, behold, I thought, he will surely come out to me, and stand, and call on the name of the Lord his God, and strike his hand over the place, and recover the leper. Are not Abana and Pharpar, rivers of Damascus, better than all the waters of Israel? May I not wash in them, and be clean? So he turned and went away in a rage. And his servants came near, and spake unto him, and said, my father, if the prophet had bid thee **do some** great thing* *would thou not had done **it***? *How much rather then, when he saith to thee, wash, and be clean? Then he went down, and dipped himself seven times in Jordan, according to the saying of the man of God: and his flesh came again like unto the flesh of a little child, and he was clean (2Kings 5:10-14).*

There are times when our only solution to wrath is execution. When someone has offended us, we sometime feel the only way of gaining satisfaction is by returning wrath for wrath. *So they hanged Haman on the gallows that he had prepared for Mordecai then was the king's wrath pacified (Esth.7:10).*

Be careful, the ditch you dig for others may be your down fall. As Haman was hanged on the gallows he prepared for Mordecai, the trap we set for others may be the one that entraps us. It's been said when you dig one ditch, dig two. Plodding evil for evil only brings wrath upon us.

Strife

Strife is defined as vigorous or bitter conflict between people. Strife is the act or state of fighting or quarreling, contention, or competition. It rises from many different sources. Lies and wrong doings are probably two of the main igniters of strife. In Proverbs 10:12 we're told, *Hatred stirs up strife* and in prov. 16:28a we see perverseness is a cause. *A perverse man sows strife and a whisperer separates the best of friends.* Some people love to see confusion among other people or groups. Their lives are in a wreck and they hate to see others happy. There's an old saying that has been around for a long time that says "misery loves company." There's also another saying I recall; it says Satan is condemned to hell and he wants as many souls possible to go alone with him. In Prov. 17:19 we read, *"He who loves transgression loves strife, **and** he who exalts his gate seeks destruction."*

One of the ways we can have peace in our lives is to follow prov. 22:10. *Cast out the scoffer **(scorner)** and contention will leave. Yes, strife and reproach will cease.* You've heard this saying before and it's scriptural.

(Prov.26:20-21)   *Where there is no wood, the fire goes out; and where **there is** no talebearer, strife ceases. **As** charcoal is to burning coals, and wood to fire, so **is** a contentious man **(or woman)** to kindle strife.* A person' pride is another way to gender strife. (Prov.28:21) *"To show partiality is not good, because for a piece of bread a man will transgress **(sin)**.* Pride is a conceited sense of one's superiority. It origin is in the devil Isa.14:12-14. Solomon says *pride **goes** before destruction and a haughty spirit before a fall.* (Prov. 16:18) A proud look and altitude can cause would be friends to stray from you.

(Phil. 2:3) ***Let** nothing **be done** through strife or vainglory; but in lowliness of mind let each esteems others better than themselves.* Among the assembly of the saints, there should be love, kindness, patience, mercy, forgiveness, and above all understanding. When church goers act like worldly people, Paul says they're still Carnal. (1 Cor. 3:3) *For ye are yet Carnal: for whereas **there is** among you envying, and strife, and divisions, are ye not carnal, and walk as men.* In 2Tim.2:24 it says the servants of the Lord must not strive over unlearned and foolish questions which gender strife but be gentle to all **men.**

Strife among the church shows weakness in Christian growth. Meekness, mercy, and love, are signs that show maturity. Paul reminds us in Titus 3 that there was a time in each of our lives that we were sometimes foolish, disobedient, and deceived, serving divers lusts and pleasures, living in malice and envy, hateful, and hating one another but after the unmerited love and mercy of God our Savior saved us by the washing of regeneration and renewing of the Holy Ghost, we were changed. Therefore none of us are fit to look down on anyone else and none of us have reasons to brawl but all of us who are saved have reasons to be thankful to God and Christ for what they have and are doing for us. Instead of striving, let us find ways to show meekness, kindness, gentleness, and love, to all men.

Seditions

Sedition is the incitement of public disorder or rebellion against an established government or any action in speech or writing, promoting such disorder or rebellion. Aaron and Miriam attempted sedition against Moses because he had married an Ethiopian woman. (Num.12:1-13) In Acts 24:5, Paul was accused of being a mover of sedition. *For we have found this man a pestilent **fellow** and a mover of sedition among all the Jews throughout the world and a ringleader of the sect of the Nazarenes:*

Satan desired to be like the most High God. (Is.14:12-15) *How art thou fallen from heaven, O Lucifer, son of the morning! **How** art thou cut down to the ground, which didst weaken the nations! For thou hast said in thine heart, I will ascend into heaven, I will exalt my throne above the stars of God: I will sit also upon the mount of the congregation, in the sides of the north: I will ascend above the heights of the clouds; I will be like the most High. Yet thou shalt be brought down to hell, to the sides of the pit.*

Barabbas was guilty of such a crime. (Luke23:18-19) Many men and women violate the statures and commandments of God every day in order to establish their own righteousness. They deny the word of God and teach others to do so too. Men and women refusing to be what God created them to be is sedition against the government of God. *In the day that God created man, in the likeness of God made he him; male and female created he them. (Gen.5:1b-2a)* God did not and do not make mistakes. If one is born a man, then that is what God intended him to be and the same goes for a woman. God is the creator, for man or woman to change what God has made them is an offense toward the authority of God.

It is said that Satan was once the highest angel in heaven. Then pride entered his heart and he lusted not to serve God but to be like the eternal God. The creature can never be equal to the creator. When an angel or man seeks to change God's laws or his plan of creation, he places himself qualified to challenge God's decisions. Satan's decision cost him and those who followed him the greatest blessing any man or angel could ever wish for. The decision of the Supreme Court to legalize same sex marriages could eventually be more devastating for mankind than it was for the third part of the heavenly host that was thrown down to destruction with Satan.

Heresies

Heresies are teachings contrary to the truth. They are religious beliefs opposed to the orthodox doctrines of a church. Any opinion opposed to established views or doctrines. They are condemned in Titus 3:10-11. *A man that is a heretic after the first and second admonition reject; knowing that he that is such is subverted, and sinneth, being condemned of himself;* a heretic is a professed believer who maintains religious opinions contrary to those of his church.

According to the apostle Peter, a person with his own self-righteous opinions can be contagious.(2 peter 2:1-2)   *But there were false prophets also among the people, even as there shall be false teachers among you, who privily shall bring in damnable heresies, even denying the Lord that bought them, and bring upon themselves swift destruction. And many shall follow their pernicious ways; by reason of whom the way of truth shall be evil spoken of.*

Many church goers knowledge of scripture today is based upon heresy. Few people take the time to read the bible for themselves. Their knowledge of God's word is based upon what they hear the preacher or someone else says. It seems they're not concerned enough about their salvation to confirm whether the things they hear are true or false. Jesus gave command for us to search the scripture for knowledge of eternal life. (St. John 5:39) a continued study of the word of God will reveal the truth to you (St. John 8:31-32). *For the lord hath a controversy with the inhabitants of the land, because there is no truth, nor mercy, nor knowledge of god in the land. By swearing, and lying, and killing, and stealing, and committing adultery, they break out, and blood toucheth blood (Hosea 4:1b-2).* When we reject God's word, God rejects us. God's word says to obey is better than sacrifice but rebellion is as the sin of witchcraft and stubbornness is as iniquity and idolatry (1Sam.15:22-23).

Take a look around you; can't you see our world today is sinking in sin like it was in the days of ancient Israel? People have no conscience against doing wrong. Even families are having a hard time getting alone with each other. So many have turned away from God; so many others have never known the Lord. Disasters are happening all around us and it seems few realize it because of mankind's constant disobedience of God's words and commandments.

Envying

Envying is resenting others success. It hinders growth among people and nations. Envying can eventually turn to jealousy and hate. Envying one another's blessings is not a sign of a Christian love. In James 3:14, it is inconsistent for Christian believers. *But if ye have bitter envying and strife in your hearts, glory not and lie not against the truth.* The apostle tells us that pretending to love one another when in fact we grudge what others have. Then, we lie against the truth. It seems the greatest love we have for one another today is expressed in words not deeds. (1 John 3:18) *My little children let us not love in words, neither in tongue; but in deeds and truth. (1 John 2:11) but he that hate his brother is in darkness, and walk in darkness, and knows not whither he goes, because that darkness hath blinded his eyes.*

In Roman 13:13, it shows carnality in our belief. *Let us walk honestly, as in the day; not in rioting and drunkenness, not in chambering and wantonness, not in strife and envying.* In Proverbs 27:4, we're told; it's powerful. *Wrath is cruel, and anger is outrageous; but who is able to stand before envy?*

Let's look at some examples of envying in the scriptures. (Gen. 4:5, 8) *But unto Cain and* his *offering he had not respect. And Cain was very wroth, and his countenance fell. And Cain talked with Abel his brother: and it came to pass, when they were in the field, that Cain rose up against Abel his brother, and slew him.* Envy drove Cain to commit murder. We descended from the same blood line as Cain and we're capable of doing the same if not worse. In Gen. 37:3-28, we see where Joseph's brothers envied him because of the favoritism his father showed for Joseph over them and the interpretations of his dreams made them envy him even worse to the point of selling their own kin into slavery. Aaron and Miriam envied Moses because he married an Ethiopian woman. (Num.12:1-2) in 1 Sam.18:6-9, Saul became wroth because the women in song gave David more praises for his victories than him.

How often do we become envious over others buying a new car, or house, or receiving a promotion on their job? We envy others accomplishments, their money, their education, their race, and even their body stature. Envying costs us friendships, robs us of blessings, but the worse thing of all, it can cause us to lose our salvation.

Murders

Murder is the unlawful killing of a human being with malice aforethought or to kill or slaughter inhumanly or barbarously. Spiritual murder is committed by spreading gossip about a fellow human being. It originates in the heart of the spreader and eventually reaches the heart of its intended victim. (Mat. 15:19) *For out of the heart proceed evil thoughts, murders, adulteries, fornications, thefts, false witness, **and** blasphemies.* The thought of murder first originates in the heart. (1 john 3:15) *Whosoever hates his brother is a murderer: and ye know that no murderer hath eternal life abiding in him.* Mat. 5:21 tells us hatred is one of the causes of murder. The penalty for murder was ordained by God in Gen. 9:6a. *"Whoso sheddeth man's blood by man shall his blood be shed:"* Each day, as our nation grows farther and farther away from the word of God, it seems to sink deeper and deeper into sin. The taking of another's life or multiples lives brings little to no simplicity from the offender(s) but the news stations and papers reporting on the incidents gain great ratings. Our rising crime waves seem to gain little effect from society or the church. As a whole, if we were concerned enough, we, especially the churches, would in unity go to God in prayer for our nation and world to be healed. (2 Chronicles 7:14) *If my people, which are called by my name, shall humble themselves, and pray, and seek m face, and turn from their wicked ways; then will I hear from heaven, and will forgive their sin, and will heal their land.*

Church people are too busy condemning world people for their wickedness to recognize that it's not worldly people that need to change but church people. God said he would heal our land if church people would turn from their evil ways and seek his face. From the beginning of the world, it has been the righteous that made the different in the sight of God. Millions, perhaps billions, in the first world were destroyed but one man's righteousness gained enough favor in the sight of God that he was willing to give mankind another chance at life. In spite of all the wickedness that was going on in the cities of Sodom and Gomorrah, God was willing to spare those cites if only ten righteous people could be found among them. As vast as the number of the Israelites that came out of Egypt was, after their hearts turned from God and he sought to slay them, it was only for the righteous of Moses, who pleaded for them, that God spared them.

God has great respect and love for the righteous but Satan has blinded and misguided them into blaming other people or things for our nation down fall. We, the church, are meant to be an example to the world of how God wants us to live. As long as we, the church, continue to allow wicked leaders to lead us astray and shut our eyes to the evils that are going on in our church congregations, God will refuse to heal our land. Our strength lies in unity. Jesus said a house divided cannot stand. If our world is to heal, we must stand together and face up to the thing or person(s) that's hindering our growth and healing. Salvation depends on our devotion and obedient to God and not on our sympathy or like for any human being.

Murder is the sixth commandment of the ten. (Exodus 20:13) Should ever the thought of murder enter our heart, we should remember Gal. 5:21. No murderer can inherit the kingdom of God.

Drunkenness

Drunkenness is the state of intoxication. A person usually becomes intoxicated by use of strong drink or wine. Drunkenness causes disorderliness (Mat. 24: 48-51); it hinders watchfulness (1 thes.5:6-7). *Therefore let us not sleep, as do others; but let us watch and be sober. For they that sleep, sleeps in the night; and they that be drunken are drunken in the night.* It causes one to be excluded from fellowship (1 Cor. 5:11). *But now I have written unto you not to keep company, if any man that is called a brother be a fornicator, or covetous, or an idolater, or a railer, or a drunkard, or an extortioner; with such a one, no, not to eat.* It excludes one from heaven (1 Cor.6:9-10). *Know ye not that the unrighteous shall not inherit the kingdom of God? Be not deceived: neither fornicators, nor idolaters, nor adulterers, nor effeminate, nor abusers of themselves with mankind, nor thieves, nor covetous, nor drunkards, nor revilers, nor extortioners, shall inherit the kingdom of god.*

The first known drunker was Noah (Gen.9:21-22*). And he drank of the wine, and was drunken; and he was uncovered within his tent. And Ham, the father of Canaan,* *saw the nakedness of his father, and he told his two brethren without.* When a man becomes drunk, he degrades himself in the sight of others. People see a hidden side of him that's not respectable. People love spreading gossip on respectable people. In Prov. 20:1 we read, *"Wine* **is** *a mocker, strong drink* **is** *raging: and whosoever is deceived thereby is not wise."* We read in Prov. 23:21 that a drunker shall come to poverty. Strong drink and wine cause spiritual leadership to error (Isaiah 28:7). *Ye cannot drink the cup of the Lord, and the cup of devils: ye cannot be partakers of the Lord table and of the table of devils (1Cor.10:21).*

Leadership as well as all respectable people should limit their intake of wine and strong drink. It will keep their character and life style from being degraded and talked about. A drunker can neither lead himself nor others to the Lord. He/she that is drunk walks a hopeless path.

Revelings

Revelings or revelries are intemperate merrymaking. Intemperate means given to or characterized by immoderate indulgence in intoxicating drink. Unrestrained: unbridled. To make merry, or be noisily festive: We see the shamefulness of revelries in Ex. 32:4-10. Paul warns Christians about engaging in the revelries as of the wicked. (Rom.13:13) *let us walk honestly, as in the day; not in rioting and drunkenness, not in chambering and wantonness, not in strife and envying. But put ye on the Lord Jesus Christ, and make not provision for the flesh, to fulfill the lusts thereof.*

We cannot serve God and mammal too. Eventually one will win over the other. Since the friendship of the world is enmity with God (Jas.4:4), it is better to serve God and live, than serve the world at the risk of losing one' salvation. A life of contentment is a life of control. 1 Thes.5:7 states *for they that sleep sleeps in the night; and they that be drunken are drunken in the night. But let us, who are of the day, be sober, putting on the breastplate (**character**) of faith and love; and for a helmet, the hope of salvation.* So often we sing or hear the song "let the world see Jesus through you". How we walk, how we talk, how we treat others, what we do, what we say, these are the things that reflects the spirit that is within us. You'll often hear this saying among church people when they want other people to do things they're afraid or too hypocritical to do themselves. You ought to stand if you have to stand by yourself. It's not a scriptural verse but one people have taken out of context to urge others in their congregation out on a limb alone. They fail to realize one person does not make up the church but it takes a body of people. When wickedness is confronted, it should be confronted by the body not a single person. Throughout the New Testament, disagreements were confronted and solved by the church or an appointed group representing and approved by the church. One person has no strength alone by his/her self but there's strength in unity.

Effeminate

An Effeminate or homosexual is a man with female traits or a woman with male traits. One having or showing qualities attributed to women unwomanly or to men unmanly. It is a result of unbelief according to Rom. 1:26-32. *For this cause God gave them up unto vile affections: for even their women did change the natural use into that which is against nature: and likewise also the men, leaving the natural use of the woman, burned in their lust one toward another; men with men working that which is unseemly, and receiving in themselves that recompense of their error which was meet. And even as they did not like to retain God in* **their** *knowledge, God gave them over to a reprobate mind,(a mind morally depraved) to do those things which are not convenient; being filled all unrighteous, fornication, wickedness, covetousness, maliciousness, full of envy, murder, debate, deceit, malignity; whisperers, backbiters, haters of God, despiteful, proud, boasters, inventors of evil things, disobedient to parents, without understanding, covenant-breakers, without natural affection, implacable, unmerciful: who knowing the judgment of God, that they* *which commit such things are worthy of death, not only do the same, but have pleasure in them that do them.*

One who is a homosexual rejects God words in order to do those things he/she takes pleasure in. Some of the traits of homosexuals are proudness, arrogance, and disrespectfulness. If the homosexuals continue in their sins, they'll only have hell fire to look forward too. Lev.18:21 states that we, as Christians, should not let any of our seed pass through the fire to Molech **(the heathen fire god).** Yet we support our children, friends, and others, who are homosexuals, knowing that God's word has stated that they who do such shall not inherit the kingdom of God. We say we're showing them love but is it love to support a person in something that will cause his/her soul to end up in hell' fire? If we truly loved them, we would tell them the evil of such practices and support them in their efforts to change. God says to us when we sins "if we confess ours sins, he is faithful and just to forgive us **our** sins, and to cleanse us from all unrighteousness (1 John 1:9.)" If we truly believe God's promise, we should accept his word. If we say that we have not sinned, we make him **(God)** a liar, and his word is not in us 1 John1:10) but at some point we must repent of our sins and accept Jesus Christ as our Savior if we ever hope to receive salvation. Satan has always taken pleasure in getting us to deny God's word. When will we stop allowing Satan to blind us with his tactics? With the same tactic he used on mother Eve, Gen. (3:1-5) he is still using on men, women, boy, and girls, today. Sadly, I say; it's still working.

*(Lev.18:22)Thou shalt not lie with mankind, as with womankind: it is abomination (**a thing hateful and disgusting**). (Lev. 20:13) If a man also **lay** with mankind, as he lieth with a woman, both of them have committed an abomination (**a thing utterly repulsive**): they shall surely be put to death: their blood shall be upon them. For this ye know, that no whoremonger, nor unclean person, nor covetous man, who is an idolater, hath any inheritance in the kingdom of Christ and of God. Let no man deceive you with vain words: for because of these things cometh the wrath of God upon the children of disobedience. (Eph.5:5-6)* When will we ever learn, wrong is wrong and no manner of talk, or selfish pretense, will make a wrong a right. God did not make men women or women men. He does not make mistakes. People choose to be

homosexuals of their own free will burning with lust rejecting the God head in order to fulfill their own evil desires.

Homosexuality was at work in the days of Lot while he was in the cities of Sodom and Gomorrah (Gen.19). During that time, we read that men desired men for pleasure over women: God destroyed those cities because of their wickedness and it should be an example to men and women today. 2Peter 2:8 states that Lot seeing and hearing their unlawful deeds vexed his righteous soul from day to day. As it was in the days of Lot, men are constantly turning that way today. The evil homosexuality brought upon the cities of Sodom and Gomorrah is vexing America today. Ever growing, becoming stronger, and few people realize it's a sin that leads to eternal damnation.

Man is the wisest mammal on earth. He was created in the image of the eternal God. Among the other creatures God created, none have committed the abomination like that of mankind. All others creatures follow the pattern God set in place for them. They realize males are males and females are females and have not strayed from that order. Only man, the wisest of all mammals, have defied God and strayed from the natural

order of nature. (Rom.1:26-32)

Thieves

A thief is a person who steals secretly or without open force. It may be he/she is a burglar, pickpocket, highwayman, robber, or false prophet. It is the eighth commandment. (Ex20:15) *Thou shall not steal.* Jesus said in St. John 10:10, *the thief cometh not, but for to steal, and to kill, and to destroy: i am come that they might have life, and that they might have it more abundantly.*

Jer.2:26 Says a thief is ashamed when he is found out. We've heard and seen that Politian, law enforcement officers, government officials, educators, and religious leaders, humble themselves shame faceless when their wrong doings are discovered. For years, if not decades, they can steal, cheat, rob, and take what belongs to others and not feel the least guilt until they're founded out. As long as no one knows their secret, they feel no guilt or sorrow.

Whoso is a partner with a thief hateth his own soul; he heareth cursing, and bewrayeth it not. (Prov. 29:24) Christians are warned against stealing. *Let him that stole* *steal no more: but rather let him labor, working with **his** hands the things which is good, that he may have to give to him that needeth (Eph.4:28).* In 1 Cor.6:10, it is one of those things that excludes one from heaven. Being a thief is one of the things that defile a man. Peter says *"let none of you suffer as a murderer, or **as** a thief, or **as** an evildoer, or as a busybody in other people's matters." (1Peter4:15)* The fourteenth verse says if we be reproached for the name of Christ, we should be happy and the sixteenth verse says if we suffer as a Christians we should not be ashamed but rather glorify God.

One of the worse places we can steal from is the church. When we steal from the church, we're not stealing from man but from God. Many false prophets steal souls for Satan that might have followed God if they only knew the truth. Of course, like Judas who carried the money bag, they take money for services not rendered or earned. In Mt.21:13 Jesus is quoted as saying *"it is written, my house shall be called a house of prayer but you have made it a den of thieves."* This he spoke describing the religious leaders during his life in the flesh while he was here on earth and it well fits many of the religious leaders of our day and time. We see many church services put more efforts on raising money than saving souls. Well do the scriptures declare that in the latter days many will depart from the faith for the love of money, the love of money is said to be the root of all evil.

Often, I've heard people say, they were playing, singing, or preaching, for the Lord but before they'll accept an appointment a certain amount of money has to be guaranteed. People who hide behind the Lord's name for profit and gain do not realize they're thieves. Though thieves are common on earth, there are not and will never be any in heaven (Mat.19-20). They and their illicit profits will someday be the property of hell. The 37th number of Psalms says," Fret not thy self because of evil doers they will soon be cut down". People who mistrust a thief coming into their home have no problems supporting one in a leadership role in the house of God. Malachi 3:8 asks the question 'will a man rob God?" Many leaders that profess to be sent by God are robbing him of souls every day by misleading and deceiving people concerning the truths of God. The sad thing is they've lied so much till they have come to believe in their own lies not knowing they've been turned over to a reprobate mind.

Covetous

Covetousness is an insatiable desire for worldly gain. Colossians 3:5 states it to be a form of idolatry. According to Eph. 5:5, a covetous man cannot expect to inherit the kingdom of God. A saint should avoid being labeled a covetousness person Eph. 5:3.

The tenth commandment warns us against covetousness. *Thou shalt not covet thy neighbor' house, thou shalt not covet thy neighbor's wife, nor his manservant, nor his maidservant, nor his ox, nor his ass, nor anything that **is** thy neighbor's (Exodus 20:17).* Covetousness can also be defined as unbridled lust for something or someone that is unlawful for you to have. Jesus says in Luke 12:15 that we should be aware of covetousness. Life consists not in the abundance of things which we possess. Even our conversations should be void of wants, wishes, and selfish desires. ***Let your*** *conversation* ***be*** *without covetousness;* ***and be*** *content with such things as ye have: for he hath said, "I will never leave thee nor forsake thee (Heb.13:5)."* God has promised to take care of the saints needs. There's no need for the righteous to steal, cheat, or lust for what others have. In Psalms 37:25

David says, *I have been young, and **now** am old; yet have I not seen the righteous forsaken, nor his seed begging bread.*

One of man's greatest dreams or covetousness is to be rich in this world. Paul says in 1 Tim.6:9-10, *but they that will be rich fall into temptation and a snare, and **into** many foolish and hurtful lusts, which drown men in destruction and perdition. For the love of money is the root of all evil: which while some coveted after, they have erred from the faith, and pierced themselves through with many sorrows.* An example is the action of Achan in Josh.7:21 which caused him, his family, and all his possessions to be destroyed in the valley of A'-chor. *When I saw among the spoils a goodly Babylonish garment, and two hundred shekels of silver, and a wedge of gold of fifty shekels weight, then I coveted them, and took them; and, behold, they **are** hid in the earth in the midst of my tent, and the silver under it.*

We covet things that later causes us sleepless nights and unnecessary worries. The first example of covenant is Eve's desire for the forbidden fruit because she saw it as being good for food, pleasant to sight, and the chance to be wise (Gen.3:6). We've learned through experiences that everything that looks good to us is not always good for us. We buy expensive houses, cars, properties, and the likes, only to later regret our decision to do so. The apostle Paul put it best when he said, *"all things are lawful unto me, but all things are not expedient: all things are lawful for me, but I will not be brought under the power of any (1Cor. 6:12)." Let your conversation be without covetousness; and be content with such things as ye have (Heb.13:5a). But godliness with contentment is great gain for we brought nothing into **this** world, **and it is** certain we can carry nothing out (1Tim.6:6-7).*

Extortioners

According to Webster and other dictionaries, an extortioner or extortionist is a person guilty of extortion. Extortion is extorting; it is sometimes applied to the exaction of too high prices. It also covers the wrongful taking of a person's money or property with his consent but by the use of threat, violence, or under color of office. There're extortionists in every walk of life. There're extortionist money lenders, mechanics, carpenters, doctors, lawyers, ministers, and even some friendships continue through means of extortion.

Paul urges Christians to avoid keeping company with extortionists in 1 Cor.6:11. A self-righteous Pharisee in St. Luke 18:11 prayed and gave thanks to God that he was not an extortionist. 1 Cor. 6:10 says extortionists will not be able to enter the kingdom of heaven. We should learn to be faithful and honest in all our dealings. Treat other people the way you would like to be treated. This is said to be the golden rule of the bible. (Mat.7:12)

Summary

It is not my intentions to frighten or belittle anyone but to open up the truth of scripture to all those who are not aware what it said concerning the works of the flesh. Since so few people read their bible and spiritual leaders rarely speaks on these subjects, I felt an overwhelming urge to reveal them to those who have a concern for eternal life. Too many good people are misled by the heresies of today's world. In a fast pace world where it seems so many worldly activities are allowed among the church congregation, few people know what is right or what is wrong. No man's friendship is worth losing your soul for.

As Joshua said to ancient Israel (Josh.24:15-20), choose you this day whom you will serve. As for me and my house, we will serve the Lord. But he stated there were certain circumstances that had to be followed to serve the Lord. There comes a time in life when we too must choose whom we will serve, the world or God but we must get to know him before we can know how to serve him. For how can you believe in whom you have not heard? And how can you hear unless you hear it from a true minister sent by God who seeks not to draw men to himself but to God (Rom. 10:14-15).

Part 3

The Fruits of the Spirit

The Fruit of the Spirit
Galatians 5:22-23

Introduction

The fruits of the spirit are the products of love. There are many level of love we're faced with. There's the love of possessions, the love of self, the love of nature, the love of others, and the love of God. Jesus said in St. John 14:15 "if ye love me, keep my commandments." Here we see Jesus based the love of God upon obedience. Therefore we're led to believe that the love of God and parents is based upon our kindness, respect, truth, and honor of the god or persons in our midst or life. In first John 5:3b, we're told God's commandments are not grievous, his commandments as the commandments and rules of our parents are not unfair. Their aim is to make us better servants of God and respectful children.

It has been stated that love means never having to say you're sorry but we're creatures born of sinful flesh and capable of and will make mistakes. Therefore we'll have many occasions in life where we'll need to say to God, parents, and others that we're sorry. When we do wrong, it will hurt; love will drive us to become bodily sorrow and if we have true love for the person or God, we will repent and ask for forgiveness. So in reality, love means being willing to say you're sorry each and every time things are committed by you that's wrong or hurtful to the character or well beings of others.

In Galatians 5:22-23, we're given a list of the fruits of the spirit. The list includes love, joy, peace, long-suffering, gentleness, goodness, faith, meekness, and temperance, against such there is no law. A Christian is known by the fruit he/she bears. The fruits of the spirit grow not out of talk but out of service.

Love

Webster defines love as a deep affection for or attachment or devotion to someone or something. 1 Cor.1-8 tells us the way of love. (Verse one**)** *Though I speak with **the** tongues of men and of angels, and have not charity, **(love)** I am become **as** sounding brass, or a tinkling cymbal.* The apostle says one may have an eloquent manner of speech with the ability to draw and influence small and large crowds but without love, being a great speaker means nothing. (Verse two) *And though I have the gift of prophecy, and understanding all mysteries, and all knowledge; and though I have all faith, so that I could remove mountains, and have not charity, I am nothing.* Love supersedes prophecy knowledge, and all understanding. (Verse four*) Charity suffers long**, and** is kind; charity envies not; charity vaunt not itself, is not puffed up, doth not behave itself unseemly, seeks not her own, is not easily provoked, thinks no evil; rejoices not in iniquity, but rejoices in the truth; bears all things, believeth all things, endures all things. Charity never fails: but whether **there be** prophecies, they shall fail; whether **there be** tongues, they shall cease; whether **there be** knowledge,* *it shall vanish away.* After all else has passed away, charity (**love)** shall survive. *(*Verse three) *And though I bestow all my goods to feed **the poor**, and though I give my body to be burned, and have not charity, it profits me nothing.* Our aim giving should be from the heart not out of guilt or selfish means or for self-glorification but out of love. Whatever spiritual service we perform, if it's not out of love, we can expect no spiritual blessings from it.

The first and great commandment of God says *"Thou shalt love the Lord thy God with all thy heart, and with all thy soul, and all thy mind and the second is like unto it, thou shalt love thy neighbor as thyself (Mat.22:37-39)."* There're no other commandments greater than these (St. Marks 12: 31b). I John 2:10 tells us as long as we have love for our brethren we abide in the light and the love within us will strengthen us against stumbling.

God is love; and he that dwells in love dwells in God and God in him. Herein is our love made perfect, that we may have boldness in the Day of Judgment: because as he is, so are we in this world. There is no fear in love; but perfect love castes out fear; because fear hath torment. He that fears is not made perfect in love. We love him because he first loved us (1 John 4:16b-19). When we love God, it is shown through the love we have for the children of God. *A new commandment I give unto you, that ye love one another; as I have loved you, that ye also love one another. By this shall all **men** know that ye are my disciples, if ye have loved one to another (St. John14:34-35).*

1John 2:5 tells us we confirm our love for him by keeping his commandments. When we pretend to know him but continue to break his commandments, we make ourselves liars. Paul tells us to walk in love. *Owe no man anything, but to love another: for he that loves another hath fulfilled the law (Rom.13:8).* St. John 8:42 tell us it's a sign of true faith. *Jesus said to them, if God were your father, ye would love me: for I proceeded forth and came from God; neither came I of myself, but he sent me.* Love is manifested through obedience according to St. John 14:15, 21 and 23. *If ye love me, keep my commandments. He that hath my commandments, and keep them, he it is that love me: and he that love me shall be loved of my father, and I will love him, and will manifest myself to him. "..... If a man loves me, he will keep my words: and my Father will love him, and we will come unto him, and make our abode with him."*

Jesus showed his love for us by dying for us. *Greater love hath no man than this that a man lay down his life for his friends (1 John 15:13).* We show our love for Jesus by being obedience and loving our fellow man. Jesus said in Mat. 5:44 for us to love our enemies, bless them that curse us, to do good to them that hate us and pray for the ones that despitefully use and persecute us. Love is the fulfillment of the law (Romans 13:10b). We show our love in different ways. When others error in their ways, telling them of their faults shows we're concerned about their salvation. Solomon tells us when we rebuke a wise man making him aware of his wrong doings, he will come to love us (Prov. 9:8a). God loves us in spite of our sins and wants us all to come to the knowledge of the truth. *" .. God commends his love toward us, in that while we were yet sinners, Christ died for us (Romans 5:8)".* Once we belong to Christ, no one or no situation shall be able to separate us from his love (Romans 8:35). It is not his desire that any of us be lost. Prov. 10:12b says love covers all sins. As God loves and have loved all of us in and out of our sins, we should find a way to love one another without showing respect of person (James 2:1).

True love has no comparison. *Set me as a seal upon thine heart, as a seal upon thine arm: for love **is** as strong as death; ... many waters cannot quench love neither can the floods drown it: if a man would give all the substance of his house for love, it would utterly be contemned (Song. 8:6ab and7).* Romans 12:9a says let love be without dissimulation **(disguise).** A person of Love does nothing to harm his neighbor. We're told to love our neighbors as we love ourselves (Romans 13:9b).

Loving others will become difficult for us to do without the love of Christ dwelling within us. Without Christ, lusts and other temptations can find ways to enter our hearts causing hurts and destructions to our well beings. One of the most common known lusts is the love of money. *For the love of money is the root of all evil: which while some coveted after, they have erred from the faith, and pierced themselves through with many sorrows. But thou, O man of God, flee these things; and follow after righteousness, godliness, faith, love, patience, meekness. Fight the good fight of faith, lay hold on eternal life, whereunto thou art also called, and hast professed a good profession before many witnesses (1 Tim. 6:9-12).*

Joy

Joy means gladness of heart. It is the second fruit of the spirit. If we're endowed with the spirit of God and Christ, there will be seen joy in our lives. Even in the midst of persecution, joy and love should be seen in our spirit. We see the evident in Stephen's spirit as he faced death (Acts 7:59-60), as Jesus did in St. Luke 23:34), and we see the love Jesus still had for Judas in spite of his betrayal (St. Mat.26:50).

Joy can be found among the counselors of peace but one void of wisdom finds his joy in folly. When God see goodness in a man, he adds to him wisdom, knowledge, and joy. Ecclesiastes reveals the principles of having joy in your living. *Go thy way, eat thy bread with joy, and drink thy wine with a merry heart; for God now accepts thy works. Let thy garments be always white; and let thy head lack no ointment. Live joyfully with the wife whom thou love all the days of the life of thy vanity, which he hath given thee under the sun, all the days of thy vanity: for that **is** thy portion in **this** life, and in thy labor which thou take under the sun. whatsoever thy hand finds to do, do **it** with thy might; for **there is** no work, nor device, nor* *knowledge, nor wisdom, in the grave, whither thou goes (Eccl. 9:7-10).* The Psalmist says *"they that sow in tears shall reap in joy." for his anger **endures but** a moment; in his favor **is** life: weeping may endure for a night, but joy **cometh** in the morning (Ps. 126:5 and 30:5).*

The Hebrew writer said *Jesus is the author and finisher of our faith who for the joy that was set before him endured the cross, despising the shame, and is set down at the right hand of the throne of God (Hebrews 12:2).* There're various ways joy is expressed. *James says "My brethren, count it all joy when ye fall into divers temptations; knowing **this,** that the trying of your faith worketh patience (James 2:1)."* Jesus said in the presence of the angels of God there is joy over one sinner that repents (St. Luke 15:10). Like John in third John 1:4, we should get great joy out of all those we help to find the Lord especially if they continue to walk in faith and truth.

Peace

Peace means freedom from war, public disturbance, harmony, serenity; calm, quiet, without conflict, law and order restored.

Secured by faith in (Is.26:3) *Thou wilt keep him in perfect peace, whose mind is stayed on thee: because he trust in thee.* Peace is the results of justification. *Therefore being justified by faith, we have peace with God through our Lord Jesus Christ (Romans 5:1).* The scriptures say, *for he is our peace, who hath made both one, and hath broken down the middle wall of partition **between us.***

In his finally words to the Corinthians, Paul urges them to continue to live in peace. *Finally, brethren, farewell, Be perfect, be of good comfort, be of one mind, live in peace; and the God of love and peace shall be with you (2 Cor. 13:11).* God is the God of peace and as we grow toward maturity we should try with all our strength to live peaceably with all men (Rom. 15:33 and 12:18).

There are diver places and groups we seek peace among. We seek peace between our neighboring countries. We work and strive for peace among our own country, individual cities and towns, our community, between families, and even within our own minds. When we achieve peace of mind, we have comfort and joy. There's no fear of danger or hurt present. Paul tells us in Romans 14:19 to follow after the things which make for peace, and things wherewith one may edify another. Peace, according to Proverbs 3:1-2, is one of the blessings given us for keeping God's commandments. *When a man's ways please the Lord, he makes even his enemies to be at peace with him (Prov. 16:7).* We see joy among the counselors of peace because a man of understanding knows how to hold his peace but proverbs say even a fool, when he holds his peace, is counted wise: **and** he that shuts his lips **is esteemed** a man of understanding (Prov. 17:28).

Isaiah declares the Lord as the maker of peace. *I form the light, and create darkness: I make peace, and create evil: I the Lord do all these* **things** *(Is.45:7).* In St. Mark 4: 39, Jesus spoke and the wind ceased and all was at peace. He is our Prince of peace. *For unto us a child is born, unto us a son is given: and the government shall be upon his shoulder: and his name shall be called Wonderful, Counselor, The Mighty God, The everlasting Father, The*

Prince of Peace. Of the increase of **his** government and peace **there shall be** no end (Is.9:6-7a).

The carnally minded has no peace but the spiritual minded has both life and peace (Rom. 8:6). Jesus is our peace and he is the one that has broken down the middle wall of partition **between us (**Eph. 2:14). Therefore in order for us to one day see Jesus, we must follow peace and holiness with all men (Heb.12:14). *Let us therefore follow after the things which make for peace, and things wherewith one may edify another (14:19). For God is not **the author** of confusion, but of peace, as in all churches of the saints (1Cor. 14:33):*

Long-suffering

Long-suffering means forbearance. It is manifested in God's description of his nature. *And the Lord descended in the cloud, and stood with him (Moses) there, and proclaimed the name of the Lord. And the Lord passed by before him, and proclaimed, The Lord, The Lord God, merciful and gracious, long-suffering, and abundant in goodness and truth (Ex. 34:5-6).*

In 2 Peter3:9, Peter tells of God's desire for man's salvation. *The Lord is not slack concerning his promise, as some men count slackness; but is long-suffering to us-ward, not willing that any should perish, but that all should come to repentance.* It is a charge Paul gave to Timothy and is left on record for all ministers to keep. *I charge **thee** (ministers and pastors) therefore before God, and the Lord Jesus Christ, who shall judge the quick and the dead at his appearing and his kingdom; preach the word; be instant in season, out of season; reprove, rebuke, exhort with all long-suffering and doctrine (2Tim.4:1-2).* It is a virtue that all preachers need.

In Ephesians 4:1-3, it is taught as a virtue that *inspires the unity of the spirit. I therefore, the prisoner of the Lord, beseech you that ye walk worthy of the vocation wherewith ye are called, with all lowliness and meekness, with long-suffering, forbearing one another in love; endeavoring to keep the unity of the Spirit in the bond of peace.* Many times we fail to show others mercy and kindness in their struggle to overcome their weakness to sin. We're so quick to forget that we too have been a victim of the bondage of sin. Paul, in warning the Romans church, makes it plain that judging one another can be and is dangerous. *"And think thou this, O man, that judges them which do such things,* **(we who judge others)** *and does the same, that thou shalt escape the judgment of God? Or despise thou the riches of his goodness and forbearance and longsuffering: not knowing that the goodness of God leads thee to repentance (Rom. 2:3-4)."* Others prayed for us and God was patience and long-suffering toward us. We should likewise do the same. His word states that it is not his desire that any of other be lost. The Psalmist declared, *"but thou, O Lord,* **art a God full of compassion, and gracious, long-suffering, and plenteous in mercy and truth (Psalm 86:15)."**

We too like the Colossians church are urged by Paul to heed to good Christians virtues. *Put on therefore, as the* *elect of God, holy and beloved, bowels of mercies, kindness, humbleness of mind, meekness, long-suffering; forbearing one another, and forgiving one another... as Christ forgave you, so also **do** ye(Col. 3:12-13)*

Goodness

Goodness means kindness, excellence, generosity, the state of being good. (Psalms 145:9). *The Lord **is** good to all: and his tender mercies **are** over all his works. The Lord **is** good, a stronghold in the day of trouble; and he knows them that trust in him (Nahum 1:7).* We see God's goodness manifested through material blessings in Mat. 5:45 and Acts 14:17. *That ye may be the children of your Father which is in heaven: for he makes his sun to rise on the evil and on the good, and sends rain on the just and on the unjust. Nevertheless he left not himself without witness, in that he did good, and gave us rain from heaven, and fruitful seasons, filling our hearts with food and gladness*

In Psalms 31:19-20, we see spiritual blessings manifested. *.**Oh** how great **is** thy goodness, which thou hast laid up for them that fear thee; **which** thou hast wrought for them that trust in thee before the sons of men! Thou shalt hide them in the secret of thy presence from the pride of man: thou shalt keep them secretly in a pavilion from the strife of tongues.* The goodness of God is shown to us through his forgiveness of our sins. *For thou,*

*Lord, **art** good, and ready to forgive; and plenteous in mercy unto all them that call upon thee (Psalm 86:5).*

In one of David's psalm of praises he portrays God as being a gracious, compassion, and merciful God whose works should please all mankind. *I will speak of the glorious honor of thy majesty, and of thy wondrous works, and **men** shall speak of the might of thy terrible acts: and I will declare thy greatness. They shall abundantly utter the memory of thy great goodness, and shall sing of thy righteousness (Psalm 145:5-9).* Though we're all urged to be good, many of us fall short of that goal in deeds. Solomon says, *"most men will proclaim everyone his goodness: but a faithful man who can find?"* Few, if any, will confess that they're evil but many will confess their goodness. Only God is truly good. *For the word of the Lord **is** right; and all his works **are done** in truth. He loves righteousness and judgment: the earth is full of the goodness of the Lord (Psalm33:4-5).*

Speaking of God's goodness concerning Zion's future king, Zechariah writes, *and the Lord their God shall save them in that day as the flock of his people: for **they shall be as** the stones of a crown, lifted up as an ensign upon his land. For how great **is** his goodness, and how* *great **is** his   beauty! Corn shall make the young men cheerful, and new wine the maids.* Yet, Paul reminds us of the necessity of respecting God's goodness. *For if God spared not the natural branches, **take heed** lest he also spare not thee. Behold therefore the goodness and severity of God: on them which fell, severity; but toward thee, goodness, if thou continue in **his** goodness: otherwise thou also shalt be cut off (Romans 11:21-22).*

Let us always keep in mind that God showed his love toward us while we were yet sinners by sending his only begotten son to die for our sins. Our obedient to his word and our promise to him is necessary in order to continue receiving God's goodness. I'm reminded of the words Joshua said to Israel. *Now therefore fear the Lord, and serve him in sincerity and in truth: and put away the gods which your fathers served on the other side of the flood, and in Egypt; and serve ye the Lord. And if it seems evil unto you to serve the Lord, choose you this day whom ye will serve (Joshua 24:14-15a).*

At some point in each of our lives, the choice of who we will serve must be faced and decided upon. We can avoid the issue for just so long. If the spirit of the Lord truly dwells within us, goodness will spread forward from our hearts.

Faith

Faith is having confidence in the testimony of another. The Hebrew writer defines it as the substance of things hoped for, the evidence of things not seen (Hebrews 11:1). *"For we are saved by hope: but hope that is seen is not hope: for what a man see, why doth he yet hope for? (Romans 8:24) "For we walk by faith, not by sight (2 Cor.5:7):"*

The apostle, James, tells us true faith is justified by our works. He states that even the devils believe that there is one God. Faith alone is dead and cannot justify our belief in God. Faith must be accompanied or followed by works or else it's in vain. He gives us an example of how Abraham's work justified his faith when he offered his son on the altar (James 2:14-24).

There are difference levels of faith. In Mat.8:5-10, Jesus describes a centurion as having great faith. In midst of a storm at sea, he found the disciples to have little faith even with him in their presence. Paul describes the relationship between him and the Roman church as mutual faith, one where both sides had confidence in the other (Romans 1:12). Again we see in Mat.17:14-21, Jesus telling the disciples it takes a certain level of faith to do certain things. *And Jesus said unto them, because of your unbelief: for verily I say unto you, if ye have faith as a grain of mustard seed, ye shall say unto this mountain, remove hence to yonder place; and it shall remove; and nothing shall be impossible unto you. Howbeit this kind goes not out but by prayer and fasting.* While we grow in the Lord, our faith should get stronger as we continue in our service to God and our fellow man. *".... Verily, I say unto you, if ye have faith, and doubt not, ye shall not only do this* **which is done** *to the fig tree, but also if ye shall say unto this mountain, be thou removed, and be thou cast into the sea; it shall be done. And all things, whatsoever ye shall ask in prayer, believing, ye shall receive (St. Mat. 21:21-22)."* Without faith, it is fruitless to think that our prayers will be answered (James 1:7).

Faith is a gift of God given to mankind. *For by grace are ye saved through faith; and that not of yourselves, **it is** the gift of God (Eph. 2:8).* True faith in God comes forth from the heart. *"... If thou shalt confess with thy mouth the Lord Jesus, and shalt believe in thine heart that God hath raised him from the dead, thou shalt be saved. For with the heart man believes unto righteousness; and with the* *mouth confession is made unto salvation (Romans 10: 9-10).* If we have truly been born again, we should be servants of righteousness. For it is written, the just shall live by faith (Romans 1:17).

Faith has been described by degrees. In 1 Tim. 1:5, it is described as been unfeigned. 1 Cor. 15: 14, 17 tell us of a faith that is vain. Mark 2:5 introduces us to united faith. James 2:22 tell us how faith wrought with works can make faith perfect. Mat. 17:20 mentions a condition of small faith. Luke 7: 6, 7 pictures a condition of humble faith. Faith has been recorded in many different categories. From great to small, from perfect to vain, from precious to holy, we have seen faith at every level.

Faith comes by hearing and hearing by the word of God (Romans 10:17). Whatsoever is not of faith is sin (Romans 14:23b). *But the scripture hath concluded all under sin that the promise by faith of Jesus Christ might be given to them that believe. But before faith came, we were kept under the law, shut up unto the faith which should afterwards be revealed. Wherefore the law was our schoolmaster **to bring us** unto Christ, that we might be justified by faith. But after that faith is come, we are no* *longer under a schoolmaster. For we are all the children of God by faith in Christ Jesus (Gal.3:22-26).*

Faith is a vital part of the armor of God. It is the shield that protects us against the fiery darts of the wicked (Eph.6:16). *But if any provide not for his own, and specially for those of his own house, he hath denied the faith, and is worse than an infidel (1 Tim.5:8). The Hebrews writer says without faith **it is** impossible to please **him (God):** for he that cometh to God must believe that he is and **that** he is a rewarder of them that diligently seek him (Heb.11:6).* Faith in Jesus requires us not to show impartiality to any. *My brethren, have not the faith of our Lord Jesus Christ, **the Lord** of glory, with respect of persons (James 2:1).* Faith is the virtue that helps us to hold on to our calling in midst of this ever growing evil generation.

In our schools, churches, communities, and elsewhere, we often quote James 2:1 but in our actions we do just the object. It seems it is easier for us to quote scripture than to live it. Just as we must have faith to please God, faith also teaches us to be truthful to ourselves. Faith encourages us to work. It is one way we show appreciation for what our Lord does and have done for us. The apostle James said it best. *Show me thy faith without thy works, and I will show thee my faith by my works (James 2: 18b).*

Gentleness

Gentleness is defined as mildness combined with tenderness. It is one of the requirements of ministers. (2 Tim.2:24) *And the servant of the Lord must not strive; but be gentle unto all **men**, apt to teach, patient.* It is also a requirement of every Christian believer. Paul told Titus as he preached and taught the servants of God to inspire them to be possessed by the spirit of goodness. (Titus 3:1-2) *Put them in mind to be subject to principalities and powers, to obey magistrates, to be ready to every good work, to speak evil of no man, to be no brawlers, **but** gentle, showing meekness unto all men.*

In one of David's songs of deliverance, he tells of God's gentleness. *Thou hast also given me the shield of thy salvation: and thy gentleness hath made me great (2 Sam.22:36).* Not only is gentleness a virtue of God but it is also a virtue of Christ. (Mat. 11:28-29). *Come unto me, all **ye** that labor and are heavy laden, and I will give you rest. Take my yoke upon you, and learn of me; for I am meek and lowly in heart: and ye shall find rest unto your souls.*

Paul commends the Thessalonians of the gentle spirit they and the church shared toward each other. *But we were gentle among you, even as a nurse cherishes her children. So being affectionately desirous of you, we were willing to have imparted unto you, not the gospel of God only, but also our own souls, because ye were dear unto us (1 Thes.2:7-8).* Gentleness is one of the fruits of the spirit and is a companion of every Christian believer. It is an unhidden virtue they can be seen in the believer's life style. As one grows older, his/her gentleness should become more apparent.

David gave thanks to God not only for his deliverance but also for his kindness of lifting him up. *Thou hast also given me the shield of their salvation: and thy right hand hath holden me up, and thy gentleness hath made me great (Psalm 18:35).*

Meekness

Meekness- patient and mild; one not inclined to anger or resentment. *Who is a wise man and endued with knowledge among you? Let him show out of a good conversation his works with meekness of wisdom Jas.3:13). Wherefore lay apart all filthiness and superfluity of naughtiness, and receive with meekness the engrafted word, which is able to save your souls (Jas.1:21).*

Jesus said that the meek shall inherit the earth (Mat.5:5). *The meek shall eat and be satisfied: they shall praise the Lord that seeks him: your heart shall live forever (Ps. 22:26).* God will guide the meek in judgment and teach them his way (Ps. 25:9). Paul tells us to use the spirit of meekness and mercy when dealing with fellow church members who have been over taken in a fault. In every case, we should consider the golden rule (do unto others as you would have them do unto you) found in St. Luke 6:31. *Brethren, if a man be overtaken in a fault, ye which are spiritual, restore such a one in the spirit of meekness; considering thyself, lest thou also be tempted (Gal. 6:1).put on therefore, as the elect of God, holy and beloved, bowels of mercies, kindness, humbleness of mind, meekness, long-*

suffering; forbearing one another, if any man have a
*quarrel against any: even as Christ forgave you, so also **do***
ye(Col.3:12-13).

Meekness is a necessity in order to fight the good fight of faith. It is one of the virtues Paul tells the man of God to follow after (1 Tim.6:11). The Christian's character warrants us to possess and show gentleness and meekness to all men (Titus 3:2) when God truly dwells in our hearts, honor and respect in and through our character can be seen with meekness and fear (2 Tim. 3:15).

Temperance

Temperance-moderation or self-restraint in action, and self- control: Temperance is also needed even in eating. *When thou sittest to eat with a ruler, consider diligently what **is** before thee: and put a knife to thy throat, if thou **be** a man given to appetite.be not desirous of his dainties: for they **are** deceitful meat (Prov.23:1-3).* In 1 Cor.7:1-9, we're told that we need temperance considering our sexual desires. Paul tells the Corinthians that temperance is needed in all things. *... Every man that striveth for the mastery is temperate in all things. Now they **do it** to obtain a corruptible crown; but we an incorruptible. I therefore run, not as uncertainly; so fight I, not as one that beateth the air: but I keep under my body, and bring **it** into subjection lest that by any means, when I have preached to others, I myself should be a castaway (1 Cor.9:25-27).*

Proverbs reveals temperance as a plus for self-control.: *He that **is** slow to anger **is** better than the mighty; and he that ruleth his spirit than he that taketh a city (Prov.1632).* It adds to spiritual growth in 2Peter 1:5-6. *And beside this, giving all diligence, add to your faith* *virtue; and to virtue knowledge; and to knowledge temperance; and to temperance patience; and to patience godliness.* When Paul stood before Felix to defend himself concerning the faith, he did it with temperance. *And as he reasoned of righteousness, temperance, and judgment to come, Felix trembled, and answered, go thy way for this time; when I have a convenient season, I will call for thee.* When we're approached, no matter the situation, we should strive to keep a character of temperance. Even when we know others are tempting to bribe or use us as Felix sought to do in Paul's case.

Summary

As every good tree of the forest provides comfort and shelter for the creatures of nature, Christians should be able and willing to provide comfort, guidance, and love for all mankind. In this age of descending Christianity, diver kinds of evil are sprouting up among our church congregations. The works of the flesh are a Christian's fore life before conversion. The fruits of the spirit come about after conversion and they becomes more apparent as one grows older in the faith.

Love is the greatest fruit a Christian can bare and the one that regulates all others. It gives season and purpose to the other fruits. Without love, the fruit of peace, joy, meekness, faith, temperance, goodness, and gentleness could serve no purpose. The scripture speaks of how in the latter days iniquity shall abound and the love of many shall wax cold (Mat.24). We can see how this can and is possible. Among the leadership of God's people today, there're bigamists, fornicators, adulterers, thieves, effeminates, extortionists, and the likes. Women are fighting over pastors within the church congregation. Pastors are molesting young girls and boys and would be

Christians are in a state of confusion. Some of those who stand representing the righteous and loving God are evil to the core. Witnessing their wrong doings, in and out of the church, some people feel they're better off at home watching the TV ministers. Satan has deceived many people into believing they can be saved at home and never has to worry about attending church services. If the risen Lord dwells in the heart of a person, the spirit will urge the person to assemble with other saints. The saved finds joy in the company of other Christian believers. The spirit is alive and will not allow us to stand still. Therefore it will drive us, if we're saved, to assemble together. Jesus said where there are two or three gathered in my name there am I in the midst of them (Mt.18:20). This leads us to realize that fellowship is essential to salvation. Don't allow the wiles of the devil to blind you into thinking you can separate from the church and still have life within. Jesus is the head of the church and the church is a group of baptized believers in Christ. The church is not one but more than one believer with Jesus in the midst. Jesus said for us to abide in him, and he will abide in us, as the branch cannot bear fruit of itself, except it abide in the vine; no more can we, except we abide in him John 15:4.

Sunday mornings worship services seem more like a stage performance than realization. In words some pastors and some so called Christians speak of their love for their congregation but their deeds do not justify that love. Today, a large percentage of pastors, rather than serve God and the members of their congregation, seek themselves to be served. Few seem to show any concern about the well beings of their congregation. They focus more on the raising of finance than the saving of souls. It is hard to see love in leaders who are constantly absence from their church pulpit on lavish vacations.

In this day and time, many people are unsure of what is right and what is wrong. With so much corruption within our governments, religious, federal, state, and city, the norm of what use to be wrong is now being said to be right. Chaos is spreading throughout the world. Murders, robbery, rapes, thief, and every evil imagination of men minds seem to be taking root. The wrath of God is being poured down upon us daily and sin is the cause of it all. Only the people of God can make a different in this world by joining together in humbleness and unity. By standing and being obedient to what they profess to be, the world will be able to see Jesus through them.

About the Author

The author is a Christian believer who believes that Christians should let the world see Jesus through the way they live and serve not the way they talk or what others wants them to do. Talk can be deceiving but works cannot be denied. Knowing that truth is within every man's reach, this author wishes that every man, woman, boy, and girl would take the time to read God's words for themselves.